Pete

The Search
for Something More

A JOURNEY TO HUMAN FULFILMENT

the columba press

First published in 2001 by
the columba press
55A Spruce Avenue, Stillorgan Industrial Park,
Blackrock, Co Dublin

Cover by Bill Bolger
Origination by The Columba Press
Printed in Ireland by Colour Books Ltd, Dublin

ISBN 1 85607 320 3

Acknowledgements
From quiet homes and first beginning,
Out to the undiscovered ends,
There's nothing worth the wear of winning,
But laughter and the love of friends …

But I will sit by my fireside,
And put my hand before my eyes,
And trace, to fill my heart's desire,
The last of all our Odysseys.
Hilaire Belloc

To all those who have helped me realise the value of 'laughter and
the love of friends' I owe the inspiration of this book. To these I
owe a great depth of gratitude. I am especially grateful to Adrian
Millar who invited me to write the book, and to Genevieve Tobin
who has been tireless in her encouragement and in being the most
helpful critic.

Contents

Introduction

There are two films which express something that seems to happen to most of us at some stage in our adult life. This is the urge to search for something more out of life than what is offered to us, for example in our work. It is as if we have reached the top of the ladder of life only to find that what is up at the top does not satisfy us in the way we had expected it would.

One of these films that illustrates a woman's search for something more is called *Shirley Valentine*. In it Shirley becomes conscious that there should be more to her life than meeting a constant round of expectations. She realises that she must do something about meeting her own basic need to follow her own deeper desires, her own dream. The opportunity to do something practical about these desires arises unexpectedly when she is given a gift of a ticket for a holiday in one of the Greek islands. When she gets there she meets someone who gives her a sense that she has a worth beyond that earned by meeting the expectations of others. She recognises that this new sense of herself is what she has been looking for and she is determined to make her own of it. So, when the time comes for her to return home she decides to remain on in Greece until her husband comes to join her. We are left to guess what happens between them as the film ends with him making his way to the hotel where she is staying.

The second film, which focuses on a man's efforts to meet his deep desires, is called, *Regarding Henry*. Henry, who is a very successful business man, is severely injured in a mugging incident. As a result, he suffers a complete loss of memory and so, like a child, he has to learn again such basic skills as how to talk and read. He is forced to let go of a position of power in which he sought to be in control not only of his own life but of the lives of those who worked for him. As a result of having to let go of this power that he had once revelled in he learns how to make his relationship with his wife and his child a priority. To his surprise he finds that this is a much more satisfying way of life than his previous one.

The mid-life crisis

What strikes us about both these stories is that for Shirley and Henry relationships become the centre of their concern where before meeting expectations and being in control had been a priority for them. As a result of this shift in their priorities we sense that both have found something much more authentic than they originally had. They have both been called to undertake a second journey as a result of a crisis which difficult circumstances in their lives have confronted them with. This is 'the mid-life crisis' that often confronts people in their thirties and forties.

The inner journey

The nature of a crisis like this is that two roads open up before us and we are challenged with choosing between them. The choice is often between making the exterior and the material world the centre of our concern or with giving pride of place to the interior world or to that of the spirit. If we choose the latter it will involve undertaking a journey into the relationships which are at the core of our inner or spirit world.

That this inner journey is central to our lives is seen from the fact that it is such an essential element of the stories people tell when they want to express the meaning of their lives. This is the conviction of Joseph Campbell, who is probably the greatest authority on those stories that are called myths. In his book, *The Hero with a Thousand Faces,* he contends that what is central to all these stories is the idea of an inner journey. This is a journey on which we become increasingly aware of our inner world and of the four relationships which are central to it. These four are the relationships we establish with ourselves, with significant people, with others and with everything in our environment.

Four calls of adult life

The invitation to enter these four relationships is described for us in the work of the psychologist Erik Erikson in what he terms the four calls of adult life. The first of these is the call to *identity* or to discover our unique self, and then as a result of this there emerges the call to *intimacy* or to make known this inmost self. Next there emerges the call to become *generative* or to be concerned for others and our environment, and finally there is the call to *integrity* which is a call to make our own of our unique inner wisdom.

Central to all these relationships, and what builds them up and maintains them, is the love or the care we receive and respond to within them. This is the reality expressed in the saying of Martin Heidegger that 'It is care that makes and sustains us.' We can see how true this is from our own experience of people who influenced our life most and the way they did this by acknowledging, accepting and affirming us.

The disaster of modernity

Rather than accepting the invitation to go on our inner journey we can decide to remain in our outer world. We are encouraged to do this today, as we live at a time when the concerns of our outer world dominate. Due to the influence of science, economics and the consumer culture, for which the exterior, material world alone is real, the inner, spirit world has become unreal and irrelevant. The effect of this neglect of our inner world is that we live in an environment where our identity, or who we *are,* is associated with what we *have* and what we *do.* In these circumstances intimacy becomes difficult when we have not got an inmost self to share. As a result our concept of being generative means that we meet the material needs of our children, for example, but we may not offer them the intimate relationship which would meet their deeper needs.

Perhaps T. S. Eliot's description of the environment we have created as a 'wasteland' may seem too strong. However his evaluation has been echoed by many people since and very convincingly in recent times by Ken Wilber in his book called *A Short History of Everything.* In it he calls the diminishment of our inner world, due largely to the influence of science, 'the disaster of modernity'. Wilber sees the reconstruction of our inner world as the main task which faces us today.

The road less travelled
The aim of this book is to provide a concrete way to reinstate our inner world in its rightful place in relation to our outer one. This will involve an inner journey on which we attempt to discover, explore and make our own of our inner world. We will look at this inner journey as an answer to the four calls of adult life as they are described by the Dutch phychologist Erik Erikson. They are the call to identity, to intimacy, to become generative and to wisdom. Answering these calls will provide a practical way to develop the four relationships which constitute our inner world.

The layout of this book
In Part 1 we will look at what is involved in undertaking our inner journey. In Part 2 we will survey the resources we need for this journey, and in Parts 3-6 we will examine in detail what we are invited to do at the different stages of our inner journey in answer to the four calls of adult life.

The central role of exercises

The focal point of each chapter of this book is the exercise. Everything in the chapter is geared towards clarifying the aim or objective of this exercise and how we might move towards attaining it. What we hope to achieve through these exercises is an experiential and interior knowledge whereas what we get from most books is an intellectual and an exterior one. To get this interior knowledge we will make use of our story and particularly the relationships which are central to it. It is in telling this story and in our experience of the feelings, intuitions and convictions it will arouse that we will access our interior knowledge.

We may find it very demanding and, therefore, off-putting to be confronted by exercises at the end of each chapter as we may tend to see a book as a source of information and ideas. However, when we want to journey into our inner world, as we do in this book, there is no better way than by doing exercises. In doing these exercises we will be following a way mapped out for us by Ken Wilber. He is one of the most authorative writers today on the need we have to reconstruct our inner world and on how we might go about doing this. In his book, *The Marriage Of Sense And Soul,* he focuses on this need to build up our inner world and to marry it and our outer one. To do this Wilber advocates that we seek what he calls 'genuine knowledge', one that is common to our outer and inner worlds. There are three strands to this knowledge, whether one is operating in the realm of sense or of soul, whether one is evaluating a scientific experiment or a mystical experience. To attain genuine knowledge we need to:

- do something like an experiment or an exercise,
- reflect on our experience of doing the exercise to become aware of the illumination we receive from it and
- check this out with others who have done the exercise and reflected on their experience.

The form the exercises take is based on fourteen or so ways of reflecting on our experience that Ira Progoff develops in his book, *At an Intensive Journal Workshop*. Through these exercises we seek to discover, explore and make our own of the richness we each possess in our personal experience.

The following are some books that stress the importance of exercises as a way of developing our inner world:

The Marriage of Sense and Soul by Ken Wilbar
At an Intensive Journal Workshop by Ira Progoff
The New Diary by Tristine Rainer
Inner Work by Robert Johnson

PART 1

Our Inner Journey

Amid so many superficial desires there is the deep urge
to go on an inner journey into the four relationships
which constitute our inner world.
Going on this journey is very difficult today,
in a world where only the outer world is seen as real.
If we are to undertake this journey,
we need to have genuine leisure in our life
or to make the time, energy and resources available
that realising our dream or deepest desire requires.

Deep *desires* invite us

    to make a decision

to create the *space*
(i.e. the time, energy and resources)

to develop the *relationships*

    that make up our inner world

An Outline of Part 1

In Chapter 1 we examine our desire for something more. This desire is to realise some aspect of our deep dream which is often dormant due to the more tangible and insistent nature of our superficial dreams.

In Chapter 2 we turn our attention to our inner journey. The essential goal of this is to expand our consciousness of the four relationships which constitute our inner world.

In Chapter 3 we look at how our outer or ego world can dominate the inner world of our essence and preoccupy us in a diminishing or destructive way.

In Chapter 4 we examine the nature of leisure as the space we make to cultivate our inner world of relationships.

In Chapter 5 we learn how to quieten and centre ourselves as an immediate preparation for entering our inner world.

CHAPTER 1

The innate desire for something more

Our desire for something more is part of our deep dream
or our call to maturity.
Since our superficial dreams
are more tangible and insistent
and tend to dominate our attention
we need to make time for our deeper ones.

Desire is the guiding star of the outlaw.
Sam Keen

What do you want?

Our superficial

Our deep dream

dreams

How much do you want it?
Does it call for a decision?

People's desire for something more in their lives can arise from a sense of frustration with the situation they find themselves in or from a need to add a new dimension to the quality of their life, They may have climbed the ladder of success and found that what is at the top of the ladder is not all that it was made out to be. This disillusionment may provide the opportunity for them to question their wisdom in selling their deep dream to the dream merchant.

The Dream Merchant

Nick is employed by a big multinational company as a dream merchant. This means that he has the unusual job of buying and selling dreams. The idea is to get people to trade in their deep dreams, which they have ceased to value, for ones that, though they are superficial, are more interesting. The reason why his company employs Nick to do this work is they realise that when people focus on their deep dream they have little or no desire for what this multinational company wants to sell them. If, on the other hand, people can be persuaded to focus on their superficial desires, they will be open to an endless stream of desire which can be stimulated by the company at will.

Sometimes Nick is a little uneasy about all of this, for he notices that when he buys someone's deep dream, the life seems to go out of them. What removes any misgivings Nick has about his work, however, is that most people are only too willing to do business with him. They obviously find their deep dream a bit unreal and irrelevant in the world in which they live.

The deep significance of some desires

When we experience a desire for something more in life we are often being put in touch with our deep dream. This dream, which is innate to all of us, is part of our basic urge to grow and reach maturity. This maturity is realised only bit by bit and what we are ripe for at any stage emerges in the form of deep desires or longings. However, these deep desires are so subtle and intangible that they are dominated by our superficial desires which are more tangible and intense.

In his book, *The Seven Habits of Highly Effective People,* Stephen Covey asks us to distinguish between the *important* and the *urgent* things we do each day. For example, making a phone call may be urgent but it is not important in the way that doing what is necessary to maintain good relationships with people is. Covey asks us to notice how some things we do are both urgent and important, some are important but not urgent, some are not important but urgent and some are neither important nor urgent. To be effective in our work and in our relationships Covey advises us to pay less attention to what is merely urgent and more to what is important. Otherwise what is urgent tends to dominate our working day while what is neither important nor urgent tends to dominate our leisure.

Because our superficial desires are so tangible and insistent they tend to get the lion's share of our time and energy, with the result that our deep desires are neglected. If we are to let our deep desires and the dream that inspires them have the space they deserve, we need *to make a decision* to pay attention to and take responsibility for them. One way of doing this is through what we call *exercises*. By exercises we mean doing things that engage our whole person and not just our mind. We seek to engage our senses in the memory of events, the feelings and intuitions these events arouse and our deep convictions about what is true and of value. By doing exercises we hope to get not just an exterior, intellectual knowledge but an interior one that is more genuine, for it involves our whole person.

The Exercise

The aim of this exercise is to clarify what you are searching for in life and to help you to distinguish your deepest desires from your more superficial ones.

1. Look at some of the advertisements you find in any popular magazine. What desires do most of them appeal to? Do any of them appeal to your deeper desires, even if they use these to arouse your more superficial ones? You might cut out an advertisements that appeals to your deeper longings and begin a book of images, which you might add to as you make your way through these exercises.

2. Among the things you desire, some are more important than others. Describe one thing that you feel driven to do that is not really necessary or important. Write down a list of the things you desire and then prioritise these by drawing a diagram in which you

put your more important desires closer to the centre of your diagram and the less important ones closer to the periphery.

3. Give an example of something you do each day that is urgent but not important. Draw a diagram in which there are four boxes. In the first box include something that is both important and urgent, in the second box include something that is important and not urgent, in the third something that is urgent and not important, and in the fourth box something that is neither important nor urgent.

4. To clarify the desire that is most important for you at present tell the story of how this desire arose or recall a period in your life when it became clear. Are there initiatives you have taken to satisfy your deep desire or your dream? Describe one of these initiatives and any feelings and insights that arose out of this experience.

CHAPTER 2

The journey our desires call us to go on

We are called to go on an inner journey
into the four relationships
on which our inner world is based
and to receive and return the love
which establishes and sustains these relationships.

There's nothing worth the wear of winning
But laughter and the love of friends
Hilaire Belloc

The inner journey is into

four relationships:

with myself,

with significant people,

with others,

and with all creation

The Sky's The Limit

There was once a poultry farmer who was given a present of an eagle's egg. He decided to experiment by putting it with some eggs a hen was hatching out. In due course the eagle emerged with the chicks and grew up with them in the very confined area of the barnyard. Even though it was never quite the same as the chickens, it adapted itself to their ways and it always thought of itself and acted as one of them. One day when it was about a year old, its eye was caught by the inspiring sight of an eagle in full flight. This caused something to stir within the young eagle. However, it was soon brought back to earth by a rooster telling it to stop stargazing and to get on with what it was meant to be doing.

Now, there are two endings to the story. One has the young eagle putting its head back down and continuing to do what it was told for the rest of its days within the very limited world of the barnyard. The other ending is that, inspired by the vision in the sky, the young eagle stretched its wings and took off into the sky. Never again was it confined to the barnyard as from then on it had the sky for its limits.

We live in two worlds

Like the eagle we also live in two worlds. In the first half of life we focus most of our attention on our outer world, on our career, getting married, setting up our home and rearing our family. The demands of these absorb most of our energies so that we have little left for anything else. In the second half of life we are called to go on an inner journey, to make the sky our limit. We are invited to make a priority of the relationships which constitute our inner world. It is in making this inner world a priority that we realise our full potential as human beings. If, like the eagle, we choose to remain within the barnyard, confined by the boundaries set by the expectations of others, we will not have the room to develop the huge potential each of us is an heir to.

In his book, *Religious Thinking from Childhood to Adolescence*, Ronald Goldman reflects on his research on the interplay of the outer and inner worlds of young people. He discovered that for them these two worlds were quite separate. He also found that the effect of this separation damaged both worlds, as the inner without the outer became unreal, while the outer world separated from the inner one lost much of its meaning.

A person who has done much to help us to understand the interplay of our two worlds is Joseph Campbell. He spent his life studying the stories people tell to express the relationship between their outer and inner worlds. In his book called *The Hero With a Thousand Faces,* he chose the idea of the inner journey as what was central to all these stories about the two worlds in which we live. Campbell observed that on this journey we become aware of, explore and take responsibility for the relationships which we are called to make the centre, not just of our inner world but of our outer one as well.

The core of our inner and outer worlds

There are four basic relationships at the core of life. There is first of all the relationship we establish with ourselves, and inseparable from this are the relationships we establish with significant people. Then there are the relationships we establish with others and finally that with everything which forms part of our environment. These four relationships are intimately connected. Our relationship with ourselves is dependent on our relationship with the significant people, for we see ourselves in their eyes. We relate with others very much as we relate with ourselves and into these relationships we incorporate all things.

Care makes and sustains us

An element which is common to all these relationships is the love or care we receive and give within them. This love has many faces but basic to all of these is a capacity to acknowledge the essential goodness of others, to accept their limitations, to appreciate their gifts and to be concerned for their welfare. It is this basic form of love or care that establishes and sustains all our relationships.

The Exercise

The aim of this exercise is to clarify what is the relationship between your outer and inner worlds and the nature of the journey into your inner world which you are invited to undertake.

1. Choose a story from a film or novel, or a theme from a song, that says something to you about the journey of self-discovery which people go on. Describe how the story or song portrayed the idea of an inner journey and say what appealed to you about the way it did this. Look for a picture for your book of images that would capture some aspect of your own journey of self-discovery that appeals to you and then choose a caption for your picture.

2. Tell the story of how you first became aware of your inner world. Has it become more important for you in recent times? Mention one aspect of this world of relationships which attracts you and one aspect of it that you resist. What signs do you notice of people you know beginning to show an interest in answering the call to undertake their inner journey?

3. To clarify what your outer and inner worlds mean for you and how they differ, choose some words and images which help you to get a clearer picture of these two worlds. Draw a diagram of two concentric circles. To the left of this diagram list some words, images and activities which you associate with your outer world. To the right of the diagram list some words, images and activities which you associate with your inner world.

4. Describe one way you might make more room in your life to follow your deepest longings or to have the sky for your limit, What is the main reason why people resist beginning their inner journey on which they discover and explore their inner world? What makes it worthwhile for them to overcome this resistance and to undertake this journey?

CHAPTER 3

Why we resist our inner journey

To go on an inner journey is difficult
in a culture where
the exterior and the material dominate
and the inner world seems unreal, irrelevant
and even an abnormal place to be.

Getting and spending we lay waste our powers
William Wordsworth

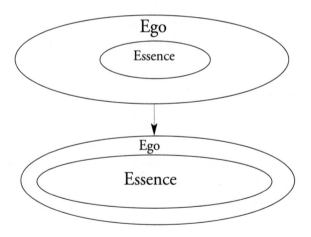

The inner and outer worlds we live in can be represented by two concentric circles. The inner circle, which represents our inner world or essence, is where we experience our deep dream and the outer circle, which represents our outer world or ego, is where we experience what is material and tangible. There is a healthy relationship between these two areas of our experience when they blend together and when each gets the attention that is its due. However, the relationship between them becomes unhealthy when one dominates and diminishes the role of the other. For example, in our relationship with our outer world we may give too much attention to our ego or outer appearance. Like the man in the following story, when we give too much attention to playing a role or meeting the expectations of others, our inner self is neglected, diminished or becomes deformed.

Playing roles that cripple us

A young man came to collect a suit his tailor had made for him. When he tried it on he noticed that one side of it was longer than the other. When he pointed this out to the tailor he was told that his suit would be a perfect fit if he held one shoulder higher than the other. The young man also noticed that one arm of the suit was longer than the other and that one leg of the trousers was too long. When he pointed this out the tailor told him that the suit would look great if he held his arm at an angle and if he walked with a limp. The tailor was so persuasive that the young man decided to wear the new suit on his way home, confident that it would create the impression he wanted to create. As he was walking through the park two old men sitting on a bench noticed him. One of them commented with sympathy on how crippled the young man was, but the other said, 'Ah yes, but what a suit!'

How this ego-domination cripples us

We can easily cripple ourselves in our effort to create the right impression. Our essence or inner world can become deformed if we neglect it by giving the bulk of our time and attention to some outer activity like work. We have so little time or energy left for cultivating our essence so that what is at the core of life fails to develop properly. We become part of the tragic situation which prevails today in which we realise only a small part of our human potential. An authoritative estimate is that we realise only 10% of our human potential and that 90% of it is unrealised. In practice, this means that we leave the fertile field of our personal experience lie fallow because we neglect what our senses, feelings, intuitions and convictions offer us.

The tragic neglect of our potential
There is surely something tragically wasteful about leaving so much potential unrealised. As the insightful Carl Jung says it is like confining ourselves to a tiny island and neglecting the riches of the ocean that surrounds us on all sides. What is truly tragic about this for Jung is that we 'remain unaware of the inner eventfulness of our lives'. We may feel that Thoreau's statement about most people leading lives of quiet desperation a bit exaggerated. However, there is a sense of deep frustration and depression that can affect people, especially in mid-life when they fail to attend to their basic needs. This is strikingly portrayed in the film *Shirley Valentine* when Shirley becomes increasingly aware of how confined her life has become. She has allowed herself to become the slave of the expectations of others and as a result she has left so much of her dream unrealised.

> 'I've led such a little life and even that will be over pretty soon. I've allowed myself to lead this little life when inside me there is so much more and it's all gone unused. And now it never will be.
>
> Why do we get all this life if we never use it? Why do we get all these feelings, and dreams and hopes? That's where Shirley Valentine disappeared, she got lost in all this unused life.'

The Exercise

The aim of this exercise is to understand the paralysing effects of your inner world being dominated by your outer one.

1. How does the story of the wonderful suit of clothes illustrate the effect of our over-preoccupation with our outer world? Choose a song, a picture, a saying or a film that illustrates the point of this story in another way. If our inner world is where we carry on our relationships, name one way in which the diminishment of this world handicaps or cripples us.

2. Describe one way that your outer world dominates your inner one by taking most of your time and energy. Make a list of the concerns that get most of your attention on an average day. Which of these gets most attention? Is there any sign that the inner world of your deep desires is asserting itself?

3. Describe an incident where someone's outer world became so dominant that the inner world of their relationships suffered. How would you want to help people like this to redress this imbalance? Is there film, a song or a proverb which would capture what you want to do or say?

4. Prepare to enter a dialogue between the inner and outer sides of yourself by briefly telling the story of each. After saying how both of these sides of you now feel about each other, begin the dialogue by letting the outer or inner side of you make an opening statement. Let the other side of you reply to this and then continue the dialogue until both sides have said all they want to. Is there a saying or an image that would capture the way the inner and outer sides of you see and feel about each other as a result of the dialogue you have engaged in?

CHAPTER 4

Leisure and the journey into relationship

Leisure is the basic requirement for our inner journey
as it makes a priority of the space
(the time, energy and resources) necessary for it.

We are active to be leisurely
Aristotle

Leisure

provides the *space,*

i.e.

the time,

the energy,

and the resources,

for our inner journey

In his book, *Leisure the Basis of Culture,* Joseph Pieper describes the situation in which we live today as one of 'total work'. By this he means that work is such a priority for many people that their life circulates around it. Pieper speaks of work being 'king' in that it rules our lives and demands a degree of dedication in terms of time and attention that leaves little for anything else. As a result, our inner world of relationships is neglected and has to survive on a subsistence diet of what time and energy is left over after work has taken its share.

In this situation where work dominates our day, we tend to be 'leisurely to be active'. Leisure becomes a pick me up, a time when we recover from the stresses and strains of work. It is not a time when we take on anything 'serious' and thus it easily becomes an escape to frivolity. However, for true leisure we need to reverse this order of priority and be, in Aristotle's words, 'active to be leisurely'.

Being active to be leisurely

In his book, *The Turning Point,* Fritjof Capra provides us with a context within which we can reappraise the importance of leisure. He sees the choice that confronts us today as being between two cultures competing for our allegiance. We are faced with deciding whether we owe our allegiance to what Capra calls 'the rising culture', which is based on relationships, or to the well-established consumer culture based on the accumulation of material things. He believes that promoting this 'rising culture' must be a matter of urgency for us as the consumer culture is proving so destructive. As Wordsworth expressed it, 'Getting and spending we lay waste our powers.'

The need to promote 'the rising culture' where relationships are a priority provides a good context for understanding the true nature of leisure and its fundamental importance for us. In this cultural context leisure is of fundamental importance for it is the space we need to provide if we are to foster the relationships which are central to our outer and inner worlds. It is from our inner world and from the relationships that are central to it that we receive what gives meaning and a sense of direction to all that goes on in our outer world. The space that leisure seeks to provide is like a secret garden.

The Secret Garden

In her book, *The Secret Garden,* Frances Burnett describes what happens when a young girl called Mary Lennox is sent to live with her uncle. She sees little of him as he is away from home most of the time and when he returns he keeps to himself as he strives to overcome his grief at the death of his wife. He has an invalid son whom he neglects and who as a result lives in virtual solitude. Mary does not know of the existance of her cousin until one night she hears crying and when she goes to discover its source she finds the room where he is confined. As the story unfolds the cousins become good friends.

Each day Mary is sent out to play by herself in the extensive gardens that surround the house. One day she discovers a hidden door that leads into a small walled garden that has been left untended for a long time. In spite of the fact that when she first discovers this secret garden it is winter and the place is desolate, she becomes attached to it. She sees in it a private place not dominated by others, where she feels at home. It is somewhere she can be herself, away from all the formality of the big house. Gradually the garden becomes more habitable and with the coming of spring it blooms and becomes a delight to the eye. But its deepest beauty is that it becomes a place where she has the space to be with her deepest self, with her cousin and eventually with her uncle.

The central role of leisure

Leisure is like this secret garden we are called to discover and to cultivate. It is a place where we can be in touch with our deepest self and with that of others. Thus leisure is for each of us the space we need to experience our deepest longings or that 'something more' we are always searching for. By space here we mean the time, the energy and the resources we need if we are to enter fully into the relationship with our deepest selves which is the basis of all our other relationships. It is the deep need we have to cultivate these relationships which makes leisure such a priority.

The major enemy of genuine leisure is our ego-dominated world. This manifests itself in the compulsive way we are inclined to devote our time, energy and resources to meeting our need for success, power, pleasure etc. These are genuine needs and remain healthy as long as they do not become a priority, for if they do they tend to imprison us or confine us to a corner of life. To be free from this ego domination that confines and imprisons us we need to make room in our life for genuine leisure. We will do this if leisure becomes sufficiently important and attractive for us. It is likely to take on this importance and attractiveness when it is seen as the space we need to answer the four calls of adult life.

Four calls of adult life
The four calls of adult life include the call to identity, to intimacy, to be generative and to integrity or wisdom. The most fundamental of these is the call to discover our *identity* or our true selves. *Intimacy* is the call to make known this true or inmost self to people like friends whom we want to become close to. When we have answered these first two calls we are then in a position to become *generative* or to answer the call to befriend others and all those areas of creation from which we may have become estranged. Finally, there is the call to *wisdom* or to savour and assimilate all we have learned from life and especially from our relationships. Understanding these four calls and how we answer them forms the core of this book.

The Exercise

The aim of this exercise is to develop a better understanding of leisure as the space you need to cultivate the relationships at the core of your life.

1. Choose a line from a song, a piece of poetry or the story of a film that illustrates for you the importance of leisure as a time to foster the relationships which mean most to you. Describe an image you have seen or choose a picture from a newspaper or magazine that highlights for you the importance of leisure and express the point the image or picture makes in a caption.

2. Draw up a list of the forms of leisure you would like to be part of your life. Get a sense of the relative importance for you of these different forms of leisure by putting some of them closer to the centre of a circle than the others. If you were more free, what place would you like leisure to have in your life?

3. List a few signs of whether work or leisure is the dominant partner in your life. If in practice leisure is for you a secondary concern, what urges you to give work such dominance? Describe a sign you have received that you need a better balance in your day between work and leisure? Name a few people whom you feel have attained a good balance in their lives between leisure and other concerns. How does this effect them? What do you admire about people who sacrifice other ambitions and choose a simple lifestyle to have more time for their relationships?

4. With a view to entering a dialogue with the side of yourself that wants to make leisure a priority, tell the story of the role leisure has played at different times in your life. Say how important leisure is for you now. Enter a dialogue between your leisurely and your active self. When you have said all you wish to, write down the main thing you want to say to each other as a result of the dialogue.

CHAPTER 5

Preparing for our journey

A very basic form of space is provided by
a quietening and centring exercise.
This facilitates our entry into the inner world

Don't just do something, says Buddha, Stand there
Daniel Berrigan

Preparing to do inner work invloves:

choosing a place

and a suitable posture

where we quieten the body

and become focused

I remember being at a course where a woman spoke strikingly about the beneficial effects on her of quietening herself in preparation for focusing on her inner world. She told us about how her two young children come to realise the good effect on her of having time apart. When they noticed that she was becoming agitated or cross they knew from past experience what had to be done. So they would gladly help her to get together what they associated with her time apart, such as her blanket, her hot water bottle and her Bible. Even though they were very young they had come to appreciate the importance for their mother of time apart as it had such a beneficial effect on her.

The importance of preparing ourselves to do inner work is emphasised by well-known psychologists like Ira Progoff, Robert Johnson and Ken Wilber. They would see that this kind of preparation has a important part to play in establishing a better balance between our outer and inner worlds. Herbert Benson, in his book *The Relaxation Response,* produces convincing evidence of the profound effect that a simple exercise for quietening and centring ourselves can have on us. He singles out four elements of this exercise that he says are common to both eastern and western traditions.

The most basic of these elements is a suitable environment. This takes the form of a time, a place and a suitable atmosphere in which we can enter our inner world. Next, we need to find a suitable posture that is both comfortable and conducive to our remaining alert. We will dwell with the third and fourth elements, which require us to quieten and to centre ourselves, in a little more detail.

Quietening ourselves and becoming focused
Learning how to quieten ourselves is a key element in entering our inner world. For example, we need to find suitable ways of lessening the tensions that the pressures we live with today easily generate. As long as we are influenced by the tension which excessive activity gives rise to, we will find it difficult to quieten ourselves.

As well as knowing how to slow down and quieten ourselves we need to develop our ability to become focused or centred. This is necessary if we are to give our attention to an inner world that is much less tangible and engaging than our outer one. Making the transition from this outer world to an inner one is difficult unless it is done gradually and in a way that engages as much of ourselves as possible. For example, we need to involve our senses, our feelings and our imagination in ways that will be suggested in the exercise to follow.

When we have quietened ourselves, we are ready to centre or focus our attention on some area of experience we wish to concentrate on. An effective way of becoming focused involves the use of a mantra. This is a brief sentence or a phrase which is used to express an experience that engages our mind and heart. For example, we might repeat a mantra like, 'Entering my inner space' or 'Taking time to be quiet'.

Different ways of quietening the body and becoming focused suit each of us. In the following exercise we will experiment with a variety of ways of entering our inner world so that we might find one which suits us.

The Exercise

The aim of this exercise is to learn how to quieten your body and how to focus your attention if you are to explore your inner world.

1. After selecting a time and a place to do your inner work, choose how you can create the right atmosphere within this space you have made. Music, a candle, a picture or image to focus on may help you to create this atmosphere.

2. Since the body has an important role to play in helping you to enter your inner world, you need to consider how best to involve it in what you want to do. For example, you need to experiment with and decide on what posture helps you. So you might find that sitting on a chair helps you to remain alert or you might find that standing is more helpful.

3. Having made space to enter your inner world and found a suitable posture you are ready to: a) quieten your body and b) focus your spirit on some aspect of your inner world.

a) Quietening your body
There follows some ways of quietening yourself that you might choose from:

Become aware of the sounds you hear around you, the more
obvious ones first and then the more subtle ones.

Become aware of any sensations you experience in one part of
your body.

Relax each part of your body in turn, letting any tension you
may notice there drain away.

Become aware of how your breathing effects your nose, stomach
or chest.

Become aware of your heartbeat, letting your experience of it
grow until it pervades your whole person.

Become aware of some feeling, letting your experience of it
expand and deepen.

If you find yourself getting diverted from what you want to
focus on, advert to this experience as perfectly normal and gently
return to what you want to focus on. If you notice signs of agitation
or disappointment growing out of your inability to remain focused,
it may indicate that you do not accept the natural limitations of
your attention span and how prone you are to become distracted.

b) Centring the spirit

When you have quietened your body you need to develop an
easy way to focus your attention. Choose some simple truth that
you are familiar with and interested in and express this in a phrase
or short sentence called a mantra. Ideally the mantra should be
short, having about seven syllables. Repeat this until you are quiet
and focused.

The main resource for our inner journey

From our memory of the significant events of our story
and from the feelings and insights they arouse
we develop a body of convictions of what is true and worthwhile
that are our main resource for our inner journey.

Our main *resource*
for our inner journey is the

sensate
feeling
intuitive
and *convictional* levels
at which we relate

and access through *memory*
and *imagination*

An outline of Part 2

In Chapter 6 we look at how we might, with the help of our memory and imagination, draw on the fund of experience we have stored in our underground stream of inner wisdom.

In Chapter 7 we examine the sensory level of our experience where we find the events of our story.

In Chapter 8 we see how influential our feelings are in the way we relate. As well as being a sign of when events are significant for us our feelings facilitate good communication.

In Chapter 9 we look at the intuitive glimpses of ourselves and others which we get from the events of our story, and how we can clarify these by articulating them.

In Chapter 10 we examine how we can convert intuitive glimpses which we get of our true significance and that of others into convictions that give our journey meaning and direction.

In Chapter 11 we examine how our imagination helps us to access the four levels of our experience, especially its depth dimension.

In Chapter 12 we focus on a body of convictions which we have accumulated throughout our lives but which are mainly dormant. Awakening these convictions is vital as they form the vision and the values which determine how alive and happy we are.

CHAPTER 6

Four levels at which we relate

The main resource we have for our inner journey
is a lifetime's experience of the four levels
at which we relate with ourselves and others.
Though this experience is mostly dormant
in our underground stream of inner wisdom,
we can gain access to its extent and depth
through our memory and imagination.

How good is man's life, the mere living! How fit to employ all the
heart and the soul and the senses, for ever in joy!
Robert Browning

Digging our well down through various levels of experience

Sensate

Feeling

Intuitive

Conviction

Our underground stream of inner wisdom
which we access through memory and imagination

How Part 1 and Part 2 are related

In Part 1 we looked at how our inner and outer worlds are related. We saw that, if their alliance is to be healthy, the four relationships that make up our inner world must become a priority. Answering the call to make these relationships a priority involves an inner journey which everyone is called to undertake in adult life. In Part 2 we want to find out more about the main resource we have for this journey. We will see that this resource consists in a huge body of wisdom that arises out of a lifetime's experience of the sensate, feeling, intuitive and thinking levels at which we relate. Unfortunately, most of this wisdom is dormant so that like the people in the following story we live permanently in a sleep-like state.

Awakenings

The story of the film called *Awakenings*, which is based on fact, is set in a psychiatric hospital in New York. The hospital is for patients who have a disease which leaves them in a sleep-like state. Even though they retain some of their basic abilities to respond to others, most of these are dormant. As the story begins an intellectually brilliant doctor comes to the hospital and through his research he finds a way of awakening the patients for short spells. During these spells they are transformed into completely different people who enjoy every aspect of life to the full. Everything they see and hear stimulates wonder, insight and strong feeling. Watching them we realise what it means to be fully alive.

By comparison the hospital staff seem to relate with each other in a very limited way. For example, the doctor seems to live in an intellectual world cut off for the most part from normal relationships with others. He is emotionally unresponsive and admits that compared to his patients his spirit is dead. By the end of the film, however, it dawns on him that his spirit has undergone an awakening. He realises, through his care for his patients and the effects of this care on them, that a whole field of experience, besides the intellectual one where he has lived most of his life, has been awakened. Even though he does not find a way of keeping his patients permanently awake, he recognises that he must find a way to nourish his own spirit by remaining alert to large areas of his life which had been dormant. The film ends with the doctor going out for a cup of coffee with a nurse who had tried, several times during the film, to awaken his heart.

Four levels at which we relate

There are four levels of our experience that tend to become dormant unless we make an effort to arouse them. We can arouse the *sensate level* of our experience by telling the story of a particular relationship or of a significant event within it. We arouse the *feeling level* of our experience when we attend to the feelings which are stimulated when we relive a part of our story. These feelings, especially if they are strong, indicate that something significant is being said to us in the event we recall. At the *intuitive level* we grasp this significance of what is said to us and at the *thinking level* of our experience we seek to make our own of the significant things that are said to us in life by converting them into convictions. It is living out of these convictions of what is true and worthwhile that makes us alive and happy like the people in the story above.

Interior knowledge

When we learn to relate with our whole person at these four levels we attain an *interior knowledge* of ourselves and others. This is very different from what we usually speak of as knowledge, which consists of information and ideas. This *exterior knowledge* does not involve our whole person but mainly our mind and is abstract and intellectual. Yet, because this exterior knowledge is much more accessible and concrete than interior knowledge, it appears more real. The result is that the interior knowledge we derive from the significant events of our story, and the feelings, intuitions and convictions these give rise to, has been neglected as somewhat unreal and allowed to become dormant.

Even though we may not be aware of it, we each possess a huge amount of interior knowledge which we have accumulated from a lifetime's experience of relationships. It is like a record written in us of how the relationships which are central to our inner world have evolved and especially of the way we have been acknowledged and accepted, appreciated and cared for within these relationships. This interior knowledge is like an underground stream of inner wisdom that runs through each person's life.

Our underground stream of inner wisdom
Our underground stream is one of inner wisdom in the sense that it is a stream of experience of all we have learned from the relationships which are central to life. It is a stream in the sense that our wisdom is an unbroken flow of personal experience stretching right from the beginning of our life up to this present moment. This stream of experience is often compared to an unbroken thread that runs from one end of life to the other. Our stream of inner wisdom is an underground stream in the sense that it is largely subconscious or runs below the surface of consciousness. We are for the most part unaware of its content because it appears unreal and unimportant compared to other kinds of knowledge. Another reason why our stream of wisdom remains underground is that bringing a lifetime's experience to the surface involves such a disciplined effort. There is also the deterrent of painful experiences being aroused when we go back to any part of our story.

The Exercise

The aim of this exercise is to appreciate the reality that the main resource you have for your inner journey is your lifetime's experience of how you have related with yourself and others.

1. List some of the ways you make use of your memory each day. Recall a film you have seen or a novel you have read in which someone loses his or her memory, and notice how it effects the person. If you were told that within the year you would lose your memory, what do you anticipate you would you miss most when you lose it? If there was one memory that you would want to write down so that you could hold onto it, what one would you choose?

2. Recall and write down a few of the more significant events of your story. Write an outline of one of these events. Dwell with one feeling aroused when you recall this event and, when you have put words on it, say these a number of times. After you have expressed in a phrase or short sentence the glimpse of yourself this event has given you, say these words a number of times. If this glimpse echoes some deep conviction or belief you have about what is true or worthwhile, see can you express it.

3. To appreciate how good a companion your memory is, recall some of the ways it helps you. Spend some time with some aspect of your memory that gives rise to a sense of wonder. After considering how your memory gives you access to your inner world by making all the richness of the past available to you, talk to it as a lifelong companion. Finally, write out the main thing you want to say to your memory and then what it says to you in reply.

CHAPTER 7

The level of our senses

The resource we have in our *senses,*
in sight, hearing, touch, taste and smell,
is like a record of life's journey written in our body.
Our relationships always remains reliant on
this most basic way we relate.

Man has no body distinct from his soul
for that called body is a portion of soul discerned by the five senses,
the chief inlets of soul in this age
William Blake

Our basic resource for our inner journey

and the foundation of all the others

is that in the events of our story we

see and are *seen,*

hear and are *heard,*

touch and are *touched,*

and thus *savour*

all that happens to us

In chapter 6 we looked at the four levels at which we relate, as these are the main resource we have for our inner journey. In this chapter we will focus on how our senses help us on this journey. They do this by enabling us to relive the events which have shaped the relationships our inner journey is all about. Our memories provide us with a box of memories that our senses help us to relive.

The Box of Memories

As an elderly couple sat together on their last night in the house they had just auctioned, it looked so bare. Just before they went to bed the husband took out a little box in which he had stored some of his most treasured memories of their life together. There were memories of the ways they had been blessed, of the joys they had shared and of their times of darkness that had turned out to be blessings in disguise. As he took these memories out of the box and as they dwelt on each one in turn, they were no longer conscious of their stark surroundings. By sharing their box of memories they relived the richness of their life together and they were grateful for all that had happened.

When he died some years later, his wife placed his box of memories between his hands as she knew that it was with these more than anything else that his spirit had been nourished. After the funeral she opened her own store of memories and placed there all the words of appreciation of her husband she had heard at the funeral. In the years that remained to her she was sustained on her solitary journey by this rich store of memories.

We are all deeply influenced by what happens in the course of our lives. The sensate level of our experience – what we see, hear, touch, taste and smell – immerses us in events in a way that has a profound and lasting effect on us. These events are the basic material out of which the tapestry of our relationships is woven. This tapestry is unique to each person, basically because the events of which it is woven are never the same for any two people.

The most basic way we relate

The importance of the sensate dimension of how we relate with others is most obvious when we are infants. Then, the affection that makes and sustains us is received through our senses and particularly through our sense of touch. When this experience of being touched or fondled is lacking, for some reason, an infant will find it difficult to relate intimately when he or she grows up. Throughout our lives so much of the care or affirmation which builds up and sustains our relationships is communicated through our senses. How important their role is can be judged from the fact that only 10% of the care we receive is communicated through words. 30% of it comes through other sounds we hear and 60% through body language or that which our senses pick up.

The foundation and root of all our experience

All the other levels at which we relate are dependent on this sensate level which acts as a foundation on which they are built, a root by which they are constantly sustained. If we fail to build on this foundation, and rely on other levels of experience to the extent that we exclude this sensate one, then our relationships will become unreal and lose an essential ingredient. It is to the events of our story that all the other levels of our experience must keep returning as to 'a mother root' if they are to remain authentic or earthed in reality.

> Who would have thought my shrivelled heart
> Could have recovered greenness? It was gone
> Quite under ground: as flowers depart
> To see their mother-root, when they have blown;
> Where they together
> All the hard weather
> Dead to the world, keep house unknown. *(George Herbert)*

It is important, therefore, to return regularly to the record that is written in our body by our senses. This is a record of events, of times and places where someone said or did something that shaped us. To lose touch with this record of events, or with our story, is to lose touch with the foundation of our relationships.

We resist reliving the events of our story

We may experience some, and perhaps a lot, of resistance to returning to the events of our story. This may be because we are afraid of opening up a painful dimension of our experience even though this may be only a small fraction of what happened. It is a pity if these painful experiences mean that we get cut off from the joy that may be ours if we return to the mainly positive events of our story. Accepting the pain and the disciplined effort of returning to the past are the price we must pay if we are to avail of the riches we possess in our box of memories. It is the memory of the care we have received in the events of our story which does so much to sustain us on our inner journey.

The Exercise

The aim of this exercise is to explore the resource you have in the sensate level at which you relate, or in your memory of events that your senses give you access to.

1. Examine an advertisement in a magazine that appeals to you and notice how many of your senses are addressed by its colours, words, etc. Notice too how it creates the atmosphere it invites you to touch and savour. How are your senses used by the stories you read in a newspaper to influence your opinion and how you feel and what you do? Which of your senses do these stories make most use of?

2. Divide your life into a number of periods and notice one significant event in each period. Take the present period of your life and write down a few events that stand out in it.

3. Write down the names of three of the most important people in your life. What comes to your attention as you remember each of these in turn? Is it what you hear them saying, what you see them doing or is it an atmosphere that surrounds them that is tangible or that you savour? Describe an experience in which you sensed your importance for someone by:

... the way he or she looked at you,

... words which were spoken to you,

... the way someone touched you

... some other gesture that you now savour.

4. Ponder for a while the role one of your senses has played in your life. Notice how many ways it is useful to you and imagine for a while what your life would be like without it. Next dwell for some time with something wondrous about this sense. Finally, after becoming aware of how you now see and feel about the sense you are focusing on, write down a few things you want to say to each other.

CHAPTER 8

The level of our feelings

Our feelings play a major role in how we relate
and are thus an important resource for our inner journey.
To draw on this resource we need to become emotionally literate,
or to notice, name and share the *feelings*
aroused by the significant events of our story.
This intensifies positive feeling,
frees us from negative ones
and leads to good communication and thus to intimacy.

Opinion is ultimately determined by the feelings,
and not by the intellect
Herbert Spencer

Noticing, naming and *sharing*

positive feelings intensifies them,

negative feelings frees us from them,

leads to good communication,

and thus to healthy relationships

The film, *The Prince of Tides* is the story of Tom Wingo and how he came to terms with his past and with the powerful feelings that the memory of it stirred up in him. There was much about the past that he loved and much that he found it hard to face. He loved his family, particularly his brother and sister, and many of the people in the small town where he grew up. He hated the endless war that went on between his mother and father and what this did to his brother and sister. Most of all he had intensely negative feelings arising from an absolutely degrading event that was the source also of his sister's suicidal despair.

As the story begins, Tom is trying to deal with the paralysing effects of his self-doubt and the deadening feelings that surround it. He knows he must come to terms with these feelings and what they are doing to himself and to his sister Savannah. She is in hospital in New York after attempting suicide. It is while Tom is there seeking to help her through her ordeal that he meets Susan Lowenstein, his sister's psychotherapist. In spite of his initial resistance to Susan's attempts to deal with his problem, she gradually gets him to unravel his feelings surrounding his past, so that by the end of the story he has come to terms with the negative feelings that have prevented him being in touch with all that was positive in his past. He gradually comes to accept all the limitations of his environment and to appreciate the fact that the good that was there far outweighed what was bad.

Being emotionally illiterate

Our tendency to ignore our feelings, as Tom did, has a diminishing effect on the way we relate. It means that we do not become as intimate with others as we feel drawn to. One of the reasons why we leave our feelings un-noticed and unspoken is that we have accepted the view that our feelings are not important, that 'they don't count'. We may also ignore our feelings because we have inherited the belief that it is better to 'leave sleeping dogs lie'. We may be convinced that bringing our feelings out into the open needlessly disturbs others. There is also a social stigma attached to being emotionally explicit as it is seen to manifest an undesirable lack of control of ourselves. The effect of this failure to express how we feel, however, is that we have become emotionally illiterate.

Benefits of becoming emotionally literate
There are a number of benefits that make it worth the effort involved in becoming emotionally literate or in developing our ability to notice, name and share our feelings. The most striking benefit is a growth in intimacy. We cannot be emotionally honest with others for any length of time without intimacy developing between us.

Another benefit of learning how to express our feelings is that we communicate more effectively, and better communications always leads to better relationships. This is the truth behind the saying that any relationship is as good as the communication going on within it. Thus, if we learn to express how we feel about what others say or do, this will greatly improve the way we relate with them. Our ability to deal with the feelings that arise in our relationships is a barometer of their healthiness.

If we pay attention to our feelings they reward us by revealing when people or circumstances are saying something significant to us. For example, the fear that we notice in a relationship may be a sign that we see the other person as a threat. On reflection, we may realise that this assumption is or is not justified and we may be in a better position to do something constructive about our fear. Not to be aware of what our feelings are saying to us means that we do not notice how unhealthy some of our reactions to people and situations are. As a result we may allow unhealthy feelings such as fear to dominate us or we may fail to cultivate healthy feelings such as gratitude.

Cultivating a healthy emotional life
Being emotionally honest involves finding a middle way between repressing our feelings and venting them with little regard for others. A healthy attention to our feelings requires that we make an effort to notice, name and share them. In this way we incorporate our negative feelings into our relationships rather than leaving them outside where they are likely to deaden if not disrupt the way we

relate. On the other hand, to pay attention to, put words on and communicate positive feelings intensifies our experience of feelings like gratitude and it also has an enlivening effect on those to whom we express feelings such as gratitude.

Feelings like anger or fear can be healthy or unhealthy. We will examine in greater depth how to deal with our unhealthy feelings in Chapter 15. Here it is sufficient to say that feelings like anger are healthy when they urge us to action in situations where some injustice needs to be dealt with. However, a feeling becomes unhealthy or negative when it is excessive or prolonged as when anger degenerates into an abiding hostility towards others. To prevent this happening we need to notice, name and share our feelings. Doing this with feelings such as anger or fear has a therapeutic effect on us. It prevents these feelings from becoming excessive or prolonged and sets us free from being dominated by them.

The Exercise

The aim of this exercise is to develop an awareness of the importance of feelings in the way you relate and as a resource for your
inner journey.

1. What is the main thing the story of the film, *Prince of Tides*,
has to say to you about the importance of being aware and taking
responsibility for your feelings? Is there another story in a novel, a
play or a film, in which people's ability or inability to handle their
feelings is central? Describe the role one feeling plays in the story
you have chosen.

2. What is the most important positive feeling for you and how
does it influence the way you relate? Describe a situation in which
it was a mistake to have left your positive feelings unspoken.
Describe an experience in which talking out your feelings in an
honest way did one of the following:
  • helped improve your communication with someone.
  • helped you become closer to someone after you had talked out
  your differences in an honest way.
  • gave you an indication of what was the underlying difficulty
  between yourself and someone else.
If it is helpful to yourself and to others to express your positive
feelings, give one reason why they are so often left unsaid?

3. What is to be said for and against the statement, 'Feelings
don't count'? Recall and re-live an event about which you have
some negative feelings. After you have noticed and named one of
these feelings, share it with yourself or with someone else. Reflect
on how this noticing, naming and sharing your negative feelings
affects you.

4. Your feelings have been your lifelong companions, playing an
important role in your life. Briefly tell the story of your relationship
with one you value taking two or three points in its development.
After saying where you stand now in your relationship, talk to each
other about how you have got on over the years. Write out the main
thing each of you wishes to say as a result of your conversation.

CHAPTER 9

The level of our intuitions

Glimpses of our significance and insignificance,
of our being acknowledged, accepted and affirmed or not,
battle for our attention.
Positive glimpses or images are limited, fleeting and fragile
so that if they are to nourish us
we need to capture them in a mantra
that is factual, personal and challenging.

A moment's insight is sometimes worth a life's experience
Oliver Wendell Holmes

Glimpses of our significance or insignificance are constructive or destructive

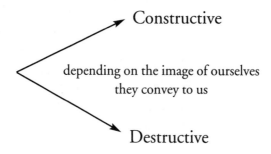

Constructive

depending on the image of ourselves
they convey to us

Destructive

The Dark Companion

The central character in Victor Hugo's novel, *The Hunchback of Notre Dame,* is a very deformed man called Quasimodo who is the bell-ringer in a monastery. He is accused of a crime he did not commit and publicly punished and reviled. When a woman from the crowd shows him compassion he finds himself accepted for the first time. This glimpse of himself that she gives him has a profound effect on him. As a result he becomes a power for good in her life and he is also the one who saves the sacred place when it is attacked by a mob intent on destroying it. The despised figure of the hunchback, once given a glimpse of himself as accepted and cared for, becomes a noble figure that we feel proud of before the story ends.

Like Quasimodo we have a mirror image of ourselves, one that is reflected back to us by the way people treat us. We are constantly being given glimpses of our significance as well as of our insignificance which we need to evaluate if we are to decide wisely who and what to believe. This decision has important implications for us as it had for Quasimodo.

Noticing when something significant is said

We need to notice when something significant is said to us. What is said to us is often not expressed directly, but in effect, and thus these important messages we receive easily go un-noticed as they are subtle and fleeting. For this reason we may live unaware of and not be nourished by the positive way others regard us.

There are a number of these ways in which people regard us positively that we might identify with. For example, people acknowledge us when, by their sensitivity to and respect for our essential goodness, they give us a sense of being significant or worthwhile. People say something important to us when they accept us in spite of our limitations. This is especially true when they see these in perspective or as a small part of the mainly good person we are. Through their appreciation people highlight the good qualities we have or the good we do. Finally, we get a glimpse of our significance when people show their practical concern for our welfare and for all we are capable of becoming.

Strong feelings are normally a good indication of when something significant is being said to us. Therefore, we need to develop an eye for these strong feelings that indicate where there is an important message for us. It is sad that we so readily pick up and become preoccupied only with the negative messages we receive and as a result let so much of what is positive and sustaining pass us by unnoticed.

Capturing the glimpses we are given

If we are to be nourished by our experience we need to develop a way of noticing, clarifying, confirming, savouring and assimilating the important glimpses we get of ourselves. When we become aware of a glimpse we have been given of ourselves we need to clarify and capture what has been said to us by putting words on our experience. The best way to do this is to express what we have glimpsed in a mantra-like statement. This statement will be most helpful to us if we allow it to be said in a personal, factual and challenging way.

The statement of what someone says to us can be put in a personal way if we allow it to be said to us face to face, in the present tense and if the person involved uses our name. The statement of what is said to us also needs to be factual or to be expressed as a fact rather than as an idea. So we might describe the idea we get of someone's care for us by saying that they are compassionate or concerned. However, this does not challenge us in the same way as allowing the person to say in a factual way, 'I am deeply concerned for you.' We need to let the significant things people say to us be said in a challenging way. We naturally prefer bland words that do not disturb the view of ourselves we are comfortable with. So it is important to let the poet in us capture our experience in words that are imaginative and that engage our feelings.

The more we allow the poet in us to struggle to express our experience in ways that are personal, factual and challenging, the clearer the glimpses we get of our significance will become. We will then be in a better position to savour and assimilate these so that they become part of a healthy vision of ourselves.

The Exercise

The aim of this exercise is to become more aware of the importance of the intuitive level at which you relate, or of the glimpses you regularly get of yourself and of others.

1. From the words of a favourite song or poem, choose something important that it is saying to you. See can you express this in a creative way that captures what is said to you in words that are interesting and enlivening as opposed to ones that are flat or banal.

2. Dwell for a short while with each of a number of people who have said something significant to you about yourself. Let what one of these people said to you be expressed in a personal way, allowing the person who said it to you to address you face to face and to use your name. Let these words be said to you a number of times until you feel at home with them. Express any good feeling this arouses or any feeling of resistance.

3. Relive an incident that happened recently in which someone said something important to you about yourself. After noticing who was present and what each of them said and did, express what was said to you in a number of ways until you hit on one that seems authentic and challenging.

4. The intuitive side of you is like a companion who is in touch with your depth dimension through images, dreams and stories. Recall an experience when you became conscious of the role of your imagination, or how it uses images or stories to speak to you and initiate a dialogue. Say how you see and feel about this intuitive side of yourself and listen to what it wishes to say to you. Write down the main thing you wish to say to each other as a result of your conversation.

CHAPTER 10

The level of our convictions

Being able to convert glimpses of our significance
into convictions that we then can savour and assimilate,
is essential to the growth of our relationships.
These convictions are easily eroded
by our failure to notice and own
the assurances of our significance which we receive.

It is not people and circumstances that upset us
but the way we see them.

Being able to convert glimpses of our significance

into convictions

is essential to our life and happiness

To be sure of our significance, and that we are worthwhile, is of the utmost importance for our relationship with ourselves and with others. Developing this sureness or level of conviction is difficult, but it is worth the effort because it has such a beneficial effect on us. There is a wonderful example of how beneficial this conviction can be in a film called, *As Good As It Gets*. It is the story of a relationship which develops between a writer and a waitress. As this relationship develops we see how he gradually comes to the following fulsome appreciation of her. We see too how reaching this conviction and expressing it effects a profound transformation in both of them.

Affirmation deserves the artful word

> I've got a great compliment for you. I might be the only person on the face of the earth that knows that you are the greatest woman on earth. I might be the only one who appreciates how amazing you are in every single thing that you do and in every single thought that you have, and how you say what you mean and how you almost always mean something that is all about being straight and good. I think most people miss that about you and I watch them, wondering how they can watch you bring their food and clear their tables and never get that they met the greatest woman alive.

Overcoming resistance

We constantly question ourselves about how significant we are in the various situations we find ourselves in. While we long to be acknowledged, accepted and appreciated we are easily put in touch with our insignificance, which is like a wound we have received and is easily re-opened. The source of this sense of insignificance and the pain it causes is often a poor self-image which has built up over the years and has become so much part of us that we hardly know what life would be like without it. People put us in touch with this poor self image not just by what they say and do but by their failure to affirm us.

However, the most common cause of our sense of a lack of self worth is our failure to notice and to own the assurance of it that we regularly receive. We are offered this assurance in the constant stream 'of little, nameless, unremembered acts of kindness and of love' (Wordsworth) which we receive from significant people such as our family and friends.

These people give us glimpses of our true worth which they invite us to believe in. What makes it difficult to believe in those who believe in us is the deeply ingrained resistance we have to listening to and assimilating the good things we hear about ourselves. Our poor self image denies or cuts down to an easily acceptable size the good that we hear about ourselves, so that little or none of it is admitted. If we do not take the necessary steps to overcome this resistance and to accept the way people acknowledge, accept and affirm us, it is likely that we will continue to earn our worth. We will use our natural gifts in manipulative ways to earn the assurance of our significance that we need.

From glimpses to convictions

What we need to do is to develop our ability not just to notice the glimpses we are given of our significance but to own them. We need to develop a practical way of converting these glimpses into convictions. The most effective way of bringing about this conversion is to go back to the significant people in our story. After singling out an incident in which something important was said to us by one of these people, we need to put words on this glimpse of ourselves which we were given. We must then dwell with these words, savouring them until we have assimilated something of what they say to us. This conversion of glimpses into convictions is a slow process because it involves a difficult change of mind and heart. This change is called for because, if we are to make room for a true or authentic way of seeing and feeling about ourselves, we need to let go of distorted ways of seeing and feeling about ourselves that are often deeply ingrained in us.

The most practical and effective way to bring about this conversion is through conversation or a dialogue. In it we listen to the good things people have said to us and then respond by expressing how we feel about these.

The Exercise

The aim of this exercise is to highlight the importance of being able to convert glimpses you get of your significance into convictions. The aim is also to discover ways of bringing about this conversion and of facing the difficulties of doing so.

1. If you were asked to choose one book, one poem and your favourite recording of one song to take with you on a period of complete solitude, what ones would you choose? Select an idea or theme from these that you feel deeply about and express this theme as briefly as you can. Tell the story of the emergence of this theme, saying when it first emerged and what it means for you now.

2. Recall an experience when you put yourself out to help someone. Imagine that this has come to the notice of a friend of yours who invites you to accept his or her appreciation of what you did. Does what they say to you echo a conviction about yourself that is important for you to remember? Record a positive feeling or one of resistance that this person's appreciation of you gives rise to.

3. Relive an incident in which something important was said to you about yourself. Express what was said in the form of a mantra that is as factual, personal and challenging as you can make it. To become more convinced of the truth of this glimpse of yourself which you have been given, say the words of the mantra repeatedly. Do you feel comfortable with them or do you resist them as unauthentic?

4. Each of us develops in the course of our life a body of convictions about what is true and about what is worthwhile. Express some of these convictions that are basic to the way you see and feel about life, to your vision and your values. Select one conviction about what is worthwhile or of value to you and that you would want to pass on to your children. Make a short statement about how it has come to mean so much to you.

CHAPTER 11

The role of our imagination

Imagination has the capacity to involve our whole person
especially in the depth dimension of the events of our story.
Through story, poetry, drama and fantasy
imagination keeps us in touch with a universal wisdom
so that we can evaluate what is healthy or not
in the way we see and feel about life.

Imagination is more important than knowledge
Albert Einstein

Imagination helps us dig our well
down through the different levels of our experience

Sensate

Feeling

Intuitive

Thinking

---

to the depth dimension of ourselves
which we can discover in our
underground stream of inner wisdom

Going Bear-hunting

There is a story told about a sociologist who was making a study of some aspects of the social life of a group of North American Indians. One day she was present when a government official was giving these people a talk on how they might improve their way of life. The sociologist noticed the leader of the group burst out laughing at a point in the talk which was not in any way amusing. She was curious about this, so after the official had gone she asked the Indian what was so amusing and in reply he said, 'Oh, at that stage the bear had just fallen into the water.' When she enquired further, she found that every time he became bored, especially by talks from government officials, he would, with the help of his imagination, go bear hunting. He said it was not quite as good as the real thing but it was an engaging substitute for such occasions.

People love stories, for through them they can have an experience of a world other than their own. Like the Indian, we may use stories to escape the ordinariness or boredom of our lives but we may also want to have the experience of being let into the lives of others, into what is going on in their minds and hearts. If the story is a challenging one, it can lead us into areas of our experience which we have not been in before but which we are now ready to enter.

The depth dimension of our experience

Our imagination, like our memory, seeks to engage our whole person. It draws us into the four levels of our experience, into the world of our senses, our feelings, our intuitions and our convictions. However, our imagination makes use of these four levels to get at a deeper aspect of our experience than our memory can. Where our memory opens up the length and breadth of our story, our imagination opens up its height and depth. Where our memory can put us in touch with our conscious world, our imagination puts us in touch with our unconscious one.

Evaluating our vision and values

Through stories, our imagination seeks to satisfy our need to be in touch with a wider world and thus to clarify what is happening in our own. A story, by putting us in touch with how other people see and feel about life, can by comparison put us in touch with how we see and how we feel. When our imagination draws us into the circumstances of another person's life we are often invited to question what we believe or to clarify and evaluate our convictions about what is true and worthwhile. Our vision and value system is aroused by our experience of that of the people in the story. We experience this, for example, in Anna Quindlen's novel *One True Thing*. In it we are faced with a situation where a mother who is dying of cancer asks her daughter to give her an overdose of the drug she is receiving to deaden her pain. This imaginary situation questions us as to what we would do if we were faced with such a dilemma.

Similarly, a fantasy about a visit to a wisdom figure may put us in touch with areas of our experience that we were unaware of. Similarly, our dreams often arouse the depth dimension of our experience through the images that spontaneously arise when we dream. For example, we may notice that we are often alone in our dreams. This image and the strong feelings it arouses may be saying something important to us about a healthy capacity we have to be alone or it may be an experience of an unhealthy tendency we have towards loneliness.

We inherit many images, ways of seeing, feeling and of evaluating the world in which we grow up. As we mature we are invited to take responsibility for the way we think and feel, for developing a healthy vision and set of values and for doing something about unhealthy ones. Our imagination provides us with a key way of doing this.

The Exercise

The aim of this exercise is to practice ways you can use your imagination to enter a depth dimension of your experience.

1. Read the following story about the tapestry-maker and then describe what bit of your inner wisdom it highlights for you:

The tapestry-maker weaves his tapestry onto a piece of gauze stretched across the centre of a room. He is on one side of this while on the other are a number of small boys, each with his own colour of thread from which the tapestry is woven. The tapestry-maker indicates where he requires the particular colour he wants to be pushed through the gauze and the little boy with that colour follows his instructions. But from time to time one of the boys loses concentration and pushes through the wrong colour or not at the place indicated. Instead of asking the boy involved to undo his mistake the master craftsman, because he is so skilled, can incorporate the mistake into his plan and even make it a feature of the tapestry.

2. Enter and get the feel of your inner room. Imagine that the centre of this room is dominated by a tapestry. This depicts your story which is expressed in much more detail by the pictures and images around the walls of this room. Look at some of these pictures and recall a few of the key moments in your story that they put you in touch with. Next, contemplate your tapestry, its colouring, its design and the images it uses to represent the most significant events and people of your life. Notice how one of these significant people or events is depicted in the tapestry. How are the limitations you have experienced and the mistakes you have made represented by darker colours for example? Is there a thread of silver or of gold running through these darker colours that represents a piece of wisdom you have learned from the difficult times you have experienced? Mention something you have learned from a time of light and something from a time of darkness that your tapestry records.

3. Your imagination has been a lifelong companion. List some of the ways that it has helped you and ponder for a while what life would be like without your imagination. After pondering for some time the wonder of how your imagination works and all the ways it is your lifelong companion, talk to it about this. Write a brief statement of the main thing you want to say to your imagination and then that your imagination wants to say in reply. When you have finished writing reflect on one thing that the exercise has helped you become aware of about your imagination.

CHAPTER 12

The growth of our vision and values

We each have a huge body of convictions
about what is true and worthwhile for us.
These express our vision and values
or the basic ways we see and feel
about ourselves and others.
On our willingness to notice and own our vision and values,
with the help of our memory and imagination,
depends how alive and happy we are going to be.

It is the most important discovery of our generation
that by changing the inner attitudes of mind
we can change all the outer aspects of our lives
William James

Happiness is an inside job

for it depends on

who and *what*

we choose to believe

Belief, however, is a hard-won conviction

In his book, *Man's Search For Meaning,* Victor Frankle's makes clear how important it is for people to find meaning in their lives. For example, he tells us that if the people he was with in the concentration camps had discovered a meaning in their lives they were more likely to survive the terrible conditions of the camps. However, finding this meaning is difficult for the events of our story may seem to be a series of disconnected facts or loose ends if we have not found the pattern that gives meaning to all these events.

The Tapestry of life

I remember once being a member of a group who were not, as a result of a lot of change, so sure of where we were going. When a new leader was taking over we asked him for some clarification about his vision for the future and about the direction in which he thought we should be moving.

In an effort to explain his position he took as an illustration the miniature tapestries his mother used to make. He explained how she used to weave a design with various colours of wool onto a piece of strong gauze. When she was finished her work there was a colourful design woven onto one side of the gauze. On the other side, however, there was a mass of disorganised loose ends.

In answer to our question our leader said that he had honestly to admit that all he could see as he took over his new job was a mass of loose ends. He felt sure, however, that if we worked together at it we would in time see something of the design. Gradually getting a sense of this design he felt sure would make what we were undertaking meaningful and give us a sense of direction.

Our lives may often appear to be a series of unconnected events with no apparent pattern or design to them. There is, however, in each person's life a distinct pattern or design, though we are mostly unaware of it. This design or meaning is discovered when we become aware of a vision or way of seeing reality that we have developed over the years. This vision of ourselves, of others and of the world around us is not an intellectual or abstract one. On the contrary, it is the fruit of the natural movement of the four levels of our experience we explored in chapters 6-11. There we saw how all the events of our story naturally move towards a vision that gives our life meaning and towards a set of values that gives it direction.

The key role of vision
There are two important aspects of our vision which we need to consider. The first of these is expressed in the saying that 'It is the vision that counts.' The truth of this may become clear from an example. You are walking along a road and in the distance you see someone approaching. Initially this person appears to be someone you are not on good terms with and as a result you begin to feel uneasy at the prospect of meeting this person. You calculate what you will do and say when you meet. However, when the person approaching draws near you realise he or she is a friend and so your feelings of unease change, giving way to ones of joyful anticipation that in turn govern your behaviour. From this example we can see that how we feel and how we act is determined or controlled to a large extent by what we see or by our vision.

Our zone of influence
Another fact which makes our vision so important is that it is within our zone of influence. This means that while we can do little to change the people and the circumstances we meet each day, we can change the way we see or perceive them. We too easily blame the circumstances and the people of our lives for our unhappiness rather than take responsibility for getting at its real source. It is not people or circumstances that upset us but the way we think about, interpret or see them.

> Two men looked out through prison bars
> One sees mud the other stars.

An all important choice of who to believe
When we go back to our story to see what it is saying to us we have to choose between focusing on the mud or the stars. We are constantly receiving messages about our significance or about our

insignificance from the way people treat us. These messages people which ask us to believe, trigger off a true or a distorted vision of ourselves. We need to decide which vision of ourselves to accept and which to reject. The glimpses that people give us of our true self need to be listened to so that they become convictions. Maintaining these convictions against the wear and tear of evidence we receive which highlights and reinforces a distorted image or vision of ourselves is a demanding task. It is, however, the price of happiness.

'The mind is its own place and can make a hell of heaven or a heaven of hell.' (John Milton)

The Exercise

The aim of this exercise is to get a practical experience of how the vision of yourself, which you choose to adopt, shapes your life.

1. Imagine that a group of people who know you well have gathered together to take part in an edition of the TV programme, *This Is Your Life*. Of those present, a brother or sister, a school friend, a work mate, your husband or wife and a close friend pay tribute to you. Listen to them as they each mention the truths you live by, your deepest concerns and what characterises the way you relate with others. After the programme go back over all that was said and pick out three things which you identify with and express how you feel about these.

2. A close friend asks you about what means most to you in life, the vision that has given your life meaning and the values that inspire the way you live. Make an outline on paper of what you would say in reply and then ask this person about the one thing he or she finds most distinctive about your vision of life, about your deepest concerns and how all this manifests itself in the way you live.

3. Imagine that you have been invited to take part in a chat show. The person who will interview you meets you beforehand and outlines what you will be asked to speak about. In preparation for the show make notes on the following:
  • an outline of where you have spent your life.
  • the major decisions you made at a number of critical times in your life to follow the unique way you have chosen.
  • what has motivated your choices and what helped you to be true to these choices especially in difficult times.
  • the most important truth about life and what is your central concern.

As you reflect on your experience of making these notes, notice how what is central to your vision and to your value system has been clarified for you and how you feel about this.

4. When did you first become aware of some aspect of the vision and of the values out of which your parents lived? Taking your mother and then your father, describe one of the truths they lived by and one value that was important for them. Express one aspect of their vision and one of their values you have adopted. Are there some of the values they held dear that you have not adopted? What part of your vision of life and what values would you like to pass on to your children? Are there many elements of your vision and the value system that are threatened by the cultural atmosphere in which you live today?

5. Are there some issues that you feel strongly about when they come up in conversation? Mention one of these points of view or one value that you find yourself concerned about. Has your conviction about this changed much over the years? Taking the present period of your life, mention one point of view or a value that you find yourself preoccupied with.

Discovering Our Identity

What is central to our vision
and the foundation of all our relationships
is our identity or the way we see ourselves.
There are two sides to our identity we must face:
the 10% that is limited and weak
and the 90% that has realised much of its rich potential.
A failure to accept our weakness
will result in a failure to appreciate our strengths.

Discovering our *identity* involves

facing two sides of ourselves,

i.e. accepting our *weaknesses*

and appreciating our *strengths*

An Outline of Part 3

In Part 3 we focus on the first call of adult life, to discover our identity. There are two aspects of this: a limited and wayward aspect which we need to accept, and an almost unlimited potential which we need to appreciate.

In chapter 13 we focus on our call to discover our identity and how it involves facing our limitations as well as appreciating our essential dignity and many gifts.

In chapter 14 we look at the crisis which the experience of our limitations gives rise to and at how these limitations can become constructive if we see them in perspective.

In chapter 15 we look at how we might deal with feelings that have become negative or destructive in that they disrupt our relationships. We look at two kinds of therapy, one for the heart and one for the mind.

In chapter 16 we focus on ways we can cultivate our true self, the self we see in the eyes of those who acknowledge, accept and affirm us.

CHAPTER 13

Discovering the two sides of ourselves

The most important reality in our
underground stream of inner wisdom is our identity
or the answer to the central question we ask ourselves,
'Are you somebody?'

We deaden the pain of a negative answer by earning a worth
that always remains limited, fragile and fleeting.
A positive answer involves accepting our limited 10%
in the light of the 90% we learn to appreciate.

Fully human people accept who they are … they know that this is
good. They know that their potential self is even greater. They are,
however, realistic about their limitations
John Powell

The call to discover our identity
involves answering the central question:

'Are you somebody?'

A healthy reply involves
accepting the limited 10%
in the light of the 90% we learn to *appreciate*

In Parts 1 and 2 we have been looking at how central relationships are to our inner journey, and also at the resources for developing these relationships which we have in the four levels at which we relate. In Part 3 we want to focus on the one relationship on which all others depend. This is our relationship with ourselves and it is the object of the first call of adult life, the call to discover our identity.

'Are you somebody?'
A well known Irish journalist, Nuala O'Faolain, entitled her autobiography, *Are You Somebody?* To explain why she chose this title she tells of an incident that occurred one day when she was in a supermarket. She describes how she noticed other customers looking at her intently thinking that they had seen her somewhere before. Eventually they came up to her and asked, 'Are you somebody?' As Nuala had appeared frequently on television she was being asked in other words, 'Haven't I seen you somewhere before?' However, the way the question was framed became the central one for her autobiography.

The central question
The question 'Are you somebody?' is one we are constantly asking ourselves. This is because our significance in the eyes of others is a primary concern for us throughout our lives. The reason this question is never far from our minds is that the answer we give to it determines to a large degree how alive and happy we are going to be.

In the opinion of those who have made a study of these matters, the answer most of us give to the question Are you somebody? is largely negative. The reason they give for this negative assessment is that in spite of seeming self-assured most people are in the grip of a poor self image. In other words, this self-assurance is often a cover for feelings of insignificance or worthlessness that are a deep-seated source of pain. Most often our reaction to this sense of insignificance and the pain it causes is that we seek to make something of ourselves or to *earn* some degree of worth that will ease or get rid of this pain. The result is that we channel an immense amount of energy into *earning* our worth rather than owning the sense of significance that the important people in our life wish to give us as a gift. However, the worth we can earn is very limited, fragile and fleeting. We have to work so hard to establish and maintain it that we have little time or energy left to find our worth in the main place it is to be found. This is in our relationships with those for whom we are truly significant.

Two aspects of our identity

To discover our true identity we need to face two aspects of it. We need to face the fact that we are weak and limited, as well as the fact that we have developed an immense amount of an almost unlimited potential which we possess. In facing these two sides of ourselves in a balanced way, it is important to realise a strange reality. This is the fact that even though our limitations are usually only 10% of who we are, they tend to dominate the image we have of ourselves. Therefore, to get a healthy picture of ourselves we need to face our limited side first of all. If we do not, our limitations will dominate our identity or the image we have of ourselves.

The Exercise

The aim of this exercise is to clarify the notion of your identity, its importance for you and how you can answer the call to discover and make your own of your true identity.

1. Choose an advertisement, a song or a story which illustrates for you how central being significant is for people. Mention one way you notice those you work with seeking their identity or trying to answer the question we constantly ask ourselves, 'Are you somebody?' What way do you seek to develop a sense of your identity or to create an image of yourself as significant?

2. Spend some time reflecting on your experience of someone who gives you a glimpse of your identity or of who you are for him or her. What did this person say and do to convey this to you? Repeat something this person said to you a number of times in a way that is challenging and personal.

3. Discovering your identity involves becoming aware of and learning to be at home with your limitations as well as with your giftedness. Write down the limitations which you identify with from the following list, and then add one or two of your own that you can think of.

a) The limitations sickness, suffering and old age impose.

b) Relationships that have not have worked out like you had hoped they would. This may be due to your own shortcomings as well as to those of others.

c) Unhealthy guilt, anger, fear or anxiety that disrupt your life.

d) How people let you down or how they fail to accept your weaknesses and to appreciate your gifts.

4. Use the following list to choose ten gifts that you value most. Is there an order of preference you would put them in?

a) Nature's gifts such as light, water and food,

b) Natural gifts such as eyesight and hearing,

c) Personal gifts you have been given in your parents, your family, your country,

d) The gift of friendship and the way that in your relationships you are acknowledged, accepted and appreciated.

When you have noticed some of these ways you are gifted, imagine what life would be like without any one of the gifts you have listed. Write down one or two things you notice as a result of doing this.

CHAPTER 14

Facing the limited side of ourselves

Awareness of our limitations causes a crisis
facing us with two options:
1) when we let the limited 10% become 90% of what we see
2) we strive to see the 10% that is limited in perspective
in the light of the 90% that is admirable.

No stranger to misery myself,
I am learning to befriend the wrteched
Virgil

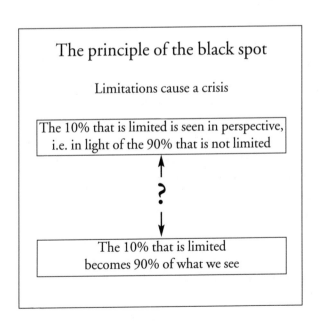

In chapter 13 we saw that we discover our identity by facing two sides of ourselves. In this chapter we focus on a way of facing the limited or shadow side of ourselves, of others and of our environment in a constructive way. The alternative is that these limitations, even though they are only a small part of who we are, will dominate the way we see ourselves and create a deadening illusion.

Cyrano de Bergerac

Cyrano de Bergerac had an unusually large nose. Unfortunately he allowed this fact to dominate the way he saw himself. So he could not accept the love of Roxanne, which he craved, because of this slight physical defect. At the end of the story, when Roxanne has developed a profound love for him one feels like saying, 'Would you not see your nose as only a slight blemish and accept her love, and all the life and happiness that it will bring you?' However, Cyrano cannot believe in her love and so he continues to live with this deadening illusion and dies a very sad and lonely man.

Our experience of limitation

Cyrano's long nose is symbolic of the way our limitations can dominate the way we see ourselves. These limitations may be physical in that they have to do with our appearance or they may be social when we allow the expectations of others to dominate us and as a result we fail to meet our own basic needs. We experience our limitations also in our weakness or moral failure when we damage or neglect our relationships. The fact that we so often fail to meet our own ideals and those of others can easily create a pervasive sense of frustration, guilt and anxiety. If something is not done about this, it erodes our worth and consequently deadens us.

The two roads limitations confront us with

Whatever form they take, our experience of our shadow side or our limitations and weakness cause a crisis in the sense that they may lead us in a constructive or in a destructive direction. In other words, our limitations and moral failure can be an invitation to grow but they can also frustrate this growth. Which direction they take us in depends largely on how we choose to view them. As we saw in chapter 12, it is our vision or our way of viewing the circumstances of our lives, and not the circumstances themselves, that determines whether or not we take the way that leads to a fuller life.

We can see the truth of this in the story of Cyrano de Bergerac. He allowed his nose to dominate the image he had of himself and this resulted in a life that was fundamentally frustrating and unhappy. But he could have seen his nose as a slight defect in the otherwise very good person that Roxanne believed him to be. If he had accepted her view of him, his physical defect could have become an invitation to be more aware of and to appreciate his nobility of character.

The constructive direction

If our limitations are to become a constructive experience we need to approach them in two ways. We need first of all to face them, as there is a temptation to deny that they are there. If we are to face our limitations, it will involve noticing, naming and sharing the feelings of frustration, guilt or sadness these limitations may give rise to. It also involves doing something about changing our way of seeing our limitations, as a distorted way of seeing them is the root cause of our negative feelings. We will examine in more detail how we deal with our feelings and with the distorted vision that causes them in the next chapter.

The second way our limitations may become a constructive experience involves learning to see them as a small part of reality that must not be allowed to dominate our whole picture of it. This small fraction of ourselves and others that is limited can become an invitation to see this shadow side of ourselves in perspective, to see the 10% of ourselves that is limited in the light of the 90% of ourselves that has almost unlimited potential, much of which has been richly realised. If we focus our attention on what is positive and see what is negative in this context, we can learn to accept and walk contentedly with life's limitations. In this way we will not allow what is defective to dominate our vision of reality but learn to see our limitations in a healthy context.

The destructive direction

What is defective in us can be symbolised by a small black spot on a sheet of white paper. We tend to see the black spot as much bigger than it is and easily allow it to capture our attention. The result is that we fail to give the white sheet of paper the attention it is due. Our tendency to become fixated with the black spot means that our limitations often take us in a destructive or unhealthy direction. We easily fall victim to three levels of illusion.

We fall victim to the first level of illusion, for example, if we get angry, and this experience gets out of proportion and colours the way we see our day. Even though the day was in fact 90% constructive, we can accept the illusion that we had a bad day. The second level of illusion takes hold of us when we allow our experience of our anger to colour the way we see ourselves and to feed our poor self image. We fall victim to the third level of illusion when our poor self image, which our anger has put us in touch with, prevents us from believing in those who believe in us. We refuse to accept their acceptance of our weakness and their appreciation of our goodness.

The Exercise

The aim of this exercise is to help you to know more about your limitations and about the constructive or destructive role they may play in your life.

1. How do the people you mix with handle their limitations? Do they face them or try to bury them, fight them or take flight from them? Choose a song or a story like that of the film, *Prince of Tides,* and describe how someone in it wrestles with his or her limitations or with those of others.

2. Make a list of some of the difficulties you have to face in your life at present and describe one of the limitations these difficulties put you in touch with. How does your experience of this limitation effect you? What way do you deal with it? What way would you like to deal with it that might be more constructive?

3. In difficult situations where you experience your shortcomings, is there a negative feeling or mood that tends to take over? What negative image of yourself does your experience of your limitations most frequently put you in touch with? What way of handling this downward spiral, in the way you see and feel about yourself, do you find helpful?

4. What constructive way of seeing life's limitations do you find helpful? Take an example of a limitation that is inclined, like a black spot on a sheet of paper, to capture your attention. After noticing, naming and walking around in the way you feel about it, see does doing this help you to accept and live more content with this limited side of yourself.

5. In order to befriend the limited and wayward side of yourself that you have become estranged from, enter into a dialogue with it in the following way. Begin by recalling some key events in the story of your relationship with this limited or wayward side of yourself. Notice any feelings or images that emerge. After saying to this weak and wayward side of yourself where you are now in your relationship with it, listen and talk to it. Write out the main thing you wish to say to each other as a result of your conversation.

CHAPTER 15

Therapy for the heart and for the mind

We need to free ourselves from destructive feelings,
such as excessive or prolonged anger, guilt, fear or anxiety
as they deaden us by feeding the illusion of our poor self image.
We may choose to do this using a therapy for the heart
or for the mind.

The therapy for the heart involves:
Talking out the negative feelings our limitations cause,
having the poor image they create accepted
and our heroic struggle with our limitations appreciated.

The therapy for the mind involves:
Using Vision Therapy to free ourselves
from a distorted vision or image of ourselves
and thus cut the roots of our negative feelings.

The mass of men lead lives of quiet desperation
Henry David Thoreau

Persistent negative feelings

like anger, guilt, fear and anxiety

need a therapy

for the *mind*

and for the *heart*

Most of the people concerned for our welfare are so anxious for us to overcome our problems that they find it hard to give us the time we need to work through them at our own pace. Like Invar in the following story, we need to be listened to in a sympathetic way if we are to be healed of life's hurts.

Talking Things Out

Invar the poet was prized by his king as much for his wise counsel as for his skill as a poet. Tragedy befell Invar when the woman he was engaged to fell in love with and married his brother. He became so depressed that he lost all his inspiration as a poet and as a counsellor. The king searched everywhere for someone who might help Invar to overcome his depression but no one was found to help him work his way through it. So the king did the little he could, which was to sit and listen to his poet's troubles each day. To everyone's surprise Invar by being allowed to talk out his sadness, broke free of his depression and regained his original inspiration.

How feelings become negative or unhealthy

Each of us carries around a body of negative feelings from our past. These feelings are negative in the sense that, though they may have been initially positive or healthy reactions to difficult situations we found ourselves in, they have become unhealthy or deadening. This is because these feelings have become excessive or prolonged. Being angry with someone from our past may have been a healthy reaction at the time in that it urged us to do something about an unjust situation. However, if we have held on to our anger beyond its time of usefulness, it is most likely a deadening influence. It may be that we were angry with someone and have never dealt with it. Instead we may have sought to bury our anger in the hope that it would cease to bother us. To the contrary, our anger is likely to remain just below the surface of consciousness and be easily triggered off by what others say or do.

As we saw in Chapter 14, the unhealthy influence of negative feelings is increased by the way they feed our poor self image, which in turn diminishes or blocks our ability to receive the acceptance and appreciation of others. The therapy we need is twofold, because it must deal with our negative feelings and with their source in some distorted image of ourselves. In other words, we need to develop a therapy for the heart that deals with our negative feelings as well as a therapy for the mind that deals with our distorted vision.

The therapy the heart needs

The therapy we need to deal with our negative feelings has three stages. The first of these involves talking out our feelings, such as anger, with a sympathetic person, who may be real or imaginary. We may need to spend some time preparing to do this by noticing the feeling that is disrupting our life and then name or find words to express it.

The second stage involves letting the person we are sharing with accept and be content with us where we are. Most people, on hearing us voice our negative feelings, are tempted to give us advice about how we might deal with our difficulties. Far from helping us, this advice may heighten our sense of inadequacy rather than ease it.

The third stage of this therapy involves letting our efforts to deal with our feelings be appreciated. This appreciation is due, for we are usually at our best or most heroic where we are struggling, and often unsuccessfully, with some area of our life. This heroism appears in the disciplined effort it takes if we are to change our mind and heart or the distorted image of ourselves and the feelings this gives rise to. It is an interesting fact that in many myths and legends people show their heroism in times of trial more than in times when everything goes smoothly.

The therapy the mind needs

A very effective means of dealing with the distorted self-image which is the root cause of much of our negative feelings is called Vision Therapy. In it we first of all seek to locate the distorted vision we want to be released from. We then encapsulate the true vision, or the correct way of seeing this situation, in a phrase or sentence and repeat this each time the negative feeling we are focusing on emerges. For example, we may feel angry because in a certain situation we feel belittled by the way someone treats us. Recognising that we are allowing their false image of ourselves to have an undue influence on us, we insert in its place a healthier one we wish to adopt. We adopt this true vision of ourselves by repeating the phrase or sentence in which we have captured it.

The Exercise

The aim of this exercise is to help you to become more aware of the kinds of persistent negative feelings that deaden you and what you can do about them.

1. What are the four most persistent negative feelings you see portrayed in the TV programmes you watch and in the films you see? Which of these negative feelings is most common among the people you mix with? Which of these feelings do you identify with? Describe a situation in which this feeling is likely to surface.

2. Tell the story of how a negative feeling has effected your life. What role does it play in your life at present and how have you learned to deal with it? Talk to the part of yourself you associate with this feeling. Write out the main thing you want to say to it and then what it wants to say to you.

3. Set out on a journey to visit someone who is a wisdom figure for you. The aim of your visit is to talk to this person about some persistent negative feeling that bothers you. As you make your way to visit this person, become aware of what you want to say and how you want to say it. When you meet your wisdom-figure, allow yourself to be led into three experiences:

a) Allow your wisdom figure to listen to you and thus to draw you into the area of negativity that bothers you. Talk to him or her about how you feel and how this effects your life.

b) Ask your wisdom figure how he or she feels about this part of your life which you feel negatively about. Notice how you feel when you are invited to accept and to walk contentedly with this limited side of yourself.

c) Let your wisdom figure ask you to be open to some words of appreciation he or she would like to say to you about the way you handle the area of your life which you have shared. For example, you may be invited to appreciate the fact that you are frequently most heroic in areas of your life where you find things most difficult. This heroism may go unnoticed by you but it is often obvious to an outside observer. Ask your wisdom figure, 'Where is the heroism that I need to appreciate in the way I am handling this area of my life which I feel is a mess?' Listen to his or her response and notice whether you accept or resist what he or she says.

4. After you have understood the following steps involved in doing Vision Therapy, see can you make use of it on some area of persistent negativity in your own life.

a) Choose an experience which is inclined to arouse strong negative feeling in you.

b) Working on the principle that it is not people and circumstances that upset us or cause negative feeling but the way we view them, see what wrong way of viewing your situation may be causing your negative feeling.

c) When you have found your false way of seeing things or your distorted vision, express in a short sentence a more realistic way of viewing the situation.

d) Each time you notice your negative feeling beginning to surface, repeat this sentence.

An example may clarify what you are being invited to do. Say for instance that you find yourself constantly frustrated by how distracted you become when you set aside time to reflect quietly on some issue. The cause of your feeling frustrated may be that you are not taking into account the fact that when you quieten yourself there are a lot of issues that jump into the quiet space that you make. You might find that words like, 'I want to live content with my humanity' may help you walk in a more realistic way with the limited side of yourself.

CHAPTER 16

Appreciating the gifted side of ourselves

Our identity or our true self is seen the eyes of others,
and especially in the eyes of significant people.
They have in the deepest sense educated us
by the quality of their acceptance and appreciation.
We need to view today's experience of our true self
in the light of our past experience of it.

Enlightenment is not an idea
but what we see in the eyes of another
Henri de Lubac

Discovering our true self

in the eyes of significant people

who care for us

is a lifelong education

in the different dimensions of this care

We have been looking at the fact that discovering our identity involves becoming aware of two sides of ourselves. There is, as we have seen, the limited side that we need to accept as well as the gifted side of ourselves that we need to affirm. This affirmation includes both an appreciation of the potential we have already realised, as well as a concern to bring what remains to be developed of this potential to full flower. This positive vision of ourselves is not an idea we get from self-analysis but a vision seen in the eyes of those who affirm us. These people, like Care in the following story, are the ones who make and sustain us by reflecting back to us a sense of our true significance or of our identity.

> ### Care makes and sustains us
> Care took some soft mud she found at the side of a river she was crossing one day and formed it into a human being. She wanted to give what she had made her own name but the *humus* or earth out of which the human being was formed also laid claim to this right. Care then asked Jupiter, who was passing by, to give what she had made a spirit. This he gladly agreed to do but then he too wanted it called after him. After arguing for some time they decided to ask Saturn to be arbiter and he gave the following decision which seemed a wise one. Jupiter had given spirit to what Care created, so he would receive that back when it died. Since it was of earth or *humus* that this human being was fashioned, it would be called a human being. However, since it was Care who formed this human being it would be her role to shape and sustain it as long as it lived.

Our sense of identity or the image we develop of our true self is built up and maintained by those who, like Care, make and sustain us. They do this by giving us a glimpse of who we are in four basic ways. We glimpse our true self in the way others acknowledge us or say in effect, 'It is good that you are.' We glimpse it too in the way they accept our limitations and weaknesses, in the way they appreciate our strengths and in their concern for our welfare.

A lifelong education

There are a number of important ways people play the role of Care when they acknowledge, accept, appreciate and are concerned about us. Our parents and family play the role of Care by their *affection* and kindness. Then perhaps when we go to school the role of Care is played by those who choose us as friends and relate with us in a more *personal* way than the members of our family may have done. From our family and friends we learn that there is a *provident,* practical and pervasive side to concern, that is shown in deeds as well as words. From those we fall in love with, and who fall in love with us, we get an experience of a love that is intense and *passionate.* If our relationship with others is *faithful,* or lasts a long time, we get an experience of a mutual acceptance and appreciation that is *profound* and *joyful.*

We each are the product, therefore, of a lifelong education by people who care for us in ways that are affectionate, personal, practical, passionate, profound, permanent and joyful. How effective this education is going to be depends on how willing we are to adopt the image of our true self the good people of our life reflect back to us. If this image of ourselves, which they want us to believe in, is to take root in us, we need to reflect on our long-term experience of it in our story and on the glimpses of it we get in the short-term each day. We will benefit most from both of these experiences of our true self if we develop a capacity to reflect on today's experience in the light of yesterday's. In other words, it is only if we learn to believe what people have revealed to us about our true self in our story that we will believe in what people reveal to us about ourselves each day.

The Exercise

The aim of this exercise is to discover your true self that is seen in the eyes of those who care for you, in the way they acknowledge, accept and affirm you in a variety of ways.

1. Make a list of the people who have influenced your life most deeply. In a word or phrase say what is distinctive about the positive

way each of the people you have listed have related with you or played the role of Care in your life.

2. Tell the story of one of these people whose relationship with you was particularly significant in that he or she gave you a sense of your significance. Briefly describe an event in which you came to realise who you were in this person's eyes. Mention one of the feelings aroused when you remember how this relationship developed. Become aware of and dwell with one insight which you treasure that this person gave you into yourself. Express this insight in words that you then let this person say to you a number of times until you feel at home with them.

3. How does dwelling with the details of your relationship with someone who means a lot to you make you feel? Besides the good feelings that surface notice ones of resistance to dwelling with what is said to you in this relationship. For example, do you notice yourself inclined to tone down expressions of praise you receive? What other form does your resistance take?

4. Do the different expressions of love that we looked at in the introduction to this exercise become important for you in a certain order during your life? Among these expressions of love are there particular ones which have a special appeal for you? Name some of the different ways people have cared for or loved you, and then select one of these ways. What was said to you in this relationship which had such a special appeal for you?

5. Look at the role Care has played in your life. Does it sound too strong to say that Care is what has made and sustained you? What words would you use to express who she is for you? Describe briefly a small number of key points in the story of your relationship with her as you gradually became aware of her influence in your life. After expressing to her what she means to you now, listen to her reply. Write down the main thing you want to say to each other.

PART 4

The Call to Intimacy

The call to intimacy
is to make known our inmost selves.
How intimate we become depends
on what we share, the depth at which we share this
and the quality of our communication.

Intimacy

or making known our inmost self

depends on

what we share

the depth at which we share it

the quality of our sharing or conversation

An Outline of Part 4

In Part 4 we examine how we can answer the second call of adult life which is to intimacy.

In Chapter 17 we examine how we answer the call to intimacy by making known or sharing our inmost self with others.

In Chapter 18 we see how conversation is the most effective and practical way of growing in intimacy.

CHAPTER 17

Making known our inner selves

Intimacy or making known our inmost selves involves:
1) the disciplined effort to know ourselves,
2) finding someone able and willing to share ourselves with and
3) providing the right atmosphere for this sharing.

How intimate we become depends on:
the content of our sharing,
the depth at which we share this
and the quality of our communication.

Friendship is the gift of self in self-disclosure
Andrew Greeley

Intimacy

or making known our inmost selves

requires that people

know themselves intimately,

share their inner selves,

by listening and responding

to each other

As well as the urge as individuals to discover our identity, or to become intimate with ourselves, there is a social urge to become intimate with others. This urge to become intimate, or to make known our inner world to another, is the second call of adult life. Answering this second call is dependent on our having answered the first call, because discovering our identity is a prerequisite for sharing it.

The difficulties of intimacy
There is a threefold difficulty involved in the sharing of ourselves with another that intimacy requires. There is the difficult task of knowing ourselves, and then that of learning how to put words on and to share this deeper side of ourselves with others. Finally, there is the difficulty of finding others who are able and willing not only to listen and respond honestly to what we have to say but who can share themselves with us as we do with them.

Most people like to talk at a superficial level, confining what they share to information and ideas. Those willing and able to communicate at a deeper level are very few, and fewer still are those willing to make the time, as well as to create the right atmosphere, in which to share. An added difficulty is the risk we take when we open ourselves to others. We are often not sure how others will react to what we reveal to them about ourselves. They may be embarrassed by what we reveal, not knowing how to react to it.

The combat of dialogue
The film called *The Horse Whisperer* is about a man who can communicate with horses. He can talk to and build up a relationship with them because he has the capacity to be sensitive to what is going on inside them. The film tells the story of how Tom uses his way with horses to overcome the effects of the trauma a horse underwent when it was involved in a horrific accident. As a result of this experience the horse refuses to let anyone come near it.

Tom has to cope not only with the horse's trauma but also with that of the young girl who was riding it at the time of the accident. She has had to deal with the shock of the accident, with having her leg amputated and with what has happened to her horse. Added to these problems Tom has to deal with what the girl's parents are going through. Like the horse and the girl, the parents are wounded and need to keep others at a distance for fear that they might touch or open up again wounds from the past.

In his struggle to draw close to the horse and to help it overcome its trauma, Tom gets engaged in the lives of the girl and her mother. In listening to them as they talk about what has driven them apart they are not only drawn closer to him but to each other.

Why we face the difficulties

The way Tom wrestles to overcome the trauma, not just of the horse but of the girl and her mother, is a symbol of how we have to struggle to overcome what keeps us apart. This is the price we pay to establish and maintain our intimate relationships, for we each come to these relationships with our own unique traumas. At he core of these is a wound caused by a sense of insignificance which events from the past have brought about. Nevertheless, in spite of the risks involved, we are willing to make the effort to disclose ourselves to others because getting close to them is an essential part of our dream – of what we long for most deeply.

Intimacy is this part of our dream that the second call of adult life invites us to realise. We all long to become intimate, to make known our inmost self to others and especially to those we love deeply. We also wish that they would give us, just as we wish to give them, that gift of self in self-disclosure in which friendship consists. There are three dimensions of this intimacy or friendship that we need to wrestle with if we are to answer fully the second call of adult life. The first has to do with the content of our sharing – the nature of what we share; the second with the depth at which we share this, and the third with the quality of our sharing or conversation.

The nature of what we share

The nature of what we share may range from factual information about, for example, our family or our work to the deepest level of ourselves which we are in touch with and are able to find words to share. It is hard to get clarity about our elusive inner world and about the relationships central to it, especially the relationship with our inmost self. We have also to struggle to find the right words with which to talk about all of this. Often the most practical obstacle to sharing ourselves at any depth is that we are not sure that others will understand or appreciate what we want to share.

The depth at which we share

Our intimacy with others also depends on the level at which we are able and willing to share. There are four of these levels which we examined in chapters 7-11. There is the sensate level at which we share the significant events of our story, and at a deeper and more revealing level we may be willing to share the feelings which are aroused when we remember these significant events. At a deeper, intuitive level we may be willing, if we are able, to share the insights into ourselves and others that we get from the events of our story and from our daily experience. At the deepest level we may be able and willing to share our convictions about what is true and what is worthwhile, our vision and our values. In sharing these we share what gives our lives meaning and a sense of direction.

The quality of our sharing

Built into each of these levels at which we share is a capacity to communicate. Our senses and intuitive powers dispose us to listen while our feelings and our convictions about what is worthwhile urge us to respond. Thus, in practice, our intimacy with others depends on how well we have developed our innate ability to listen and respond – on our ability to communicate. As this communication, conversation or dialogue is the most effective and practical way of becoming intimate we will devote chapter 18 to it.

The Exercise

The aim of this exercise is that you would have a better understanding of the nature of intimacy, its value, the difficulties involved in attaining it and how you might overcome these.

1. Choose a song, a novel, a film or a play which presents an appealing picture of intimacy. What way is intimacy presented in it? Are there ways of portraying intimacy in TV programmes or in advertisements that seem artificial to you? What requirement for intimacy is lacking in these programmes or advertisements.

2. List some people with whom you have attained some degree of intimacy. What do you share with each of these people that forms the basis of your intimacy? What makes some of these relationships more intimate than others? Spend some time with the deepest of these relationships you have been reflecting on and notice what you share within it and how you share this.

3. Tell the story of an intimate relationship you had or have, recalling when you first met the person involved and some significant experiences in the development of your relationship. As you recall these times, notice and name one of the feelings which the memory of these times arouses. As you reflect on this relationship put words on the main thing that was said to you within it. Listen to these words being said to you a number of times and then describe what effect this has on you.

4. On your way to becoming more intimate with others, you are probably aware of peak and valley periods, times when you feel involved and times when you feel at a distance from those with whom you normally feel intimate. What role do the times when you feel separated from a friend, either physically or emotionally, have to play in the development of your relationship? What truth is there for you in the saying that a relationship grows best in winter? Describe an incident when a row you had with a friend led to a new level of intimacy and an incident when you remained at the emotional distance the row led to.

5. In each of us there is a self that longs for intimacy. Tell the story in broad outline of the emergence of your desire for intimacy. Say how you now see and how you feel about this side of yourself and then enter into a dialogue with it. When the dialogue is finished, write down the main thing that each of you wants to say to the other.

CHAPTER 18

The role of conversation in intimacy

Conversation is the most effective and practical way to intimacy

It is *effective* because
by listening and responding in conversation
we develop the four levels at which we become intimate

It is *practical* because
when we listen and respond to each other in conversation
we cannot avoid becoming intimate.

A relationship is as good as the communication
going on within it

Conversation

in which we both *listen* and *respond*

is the most *effective* and *practical* way to intimacy

The price of intimacy

In the film, *Peter's Friends,* we have the story of seven people who, when they were at college, had spent a lot of time together as part of a song and dance group. The film takes place ten years later when Peter who, on inheriting a beautiful old house, decides to bring them all together again for a New Year weekend.

Their stories unfold as they take up the threads of their carefree relationships as students. Even though at the beginning of the film things seem to have worked out well for them, it soon emerges that there is a lot that has not. They have all experienced their limitations and failures and we gradually become aware that there is a lot of pain and frustration in their lives. They have tried to escape from this pain and frustration by having affairs and through their work. So, after the forced joviality of their initial reunion, hostilities emerge as they tread on each others' sensibilities and open up old wounds.

As the film progresses, they begin to climb back out of the darker side of their lives and to pick up the threads of their friendship at a deeper level. The catalyst for this upturn in their relationship is Peter's revelation of his own personal tragedy and the heroic way he has learned to face it. Peter's humble heroism opens up in the others a deep sense of compassion for him and subsequently for each other.

What facilitates this growing intimacy is the conversation they gradually get engaged in. Initially they are mainly interested in creating a good impression by talking about what they each have achieved, but gradually they become more honest. With Peter's personal revelation they are given permission, as it were, to say exactly how they feel and to listen to each other in a more sympathetic way. They have in a sense to learn how to fight, as it is in this 'combat of dialogue' that they attain a new level of intimacy.

'Only if we learn to fight'

Someone who is professionally involved in marriage counselling has written about the importance for married people of learning how to fight. The kind of fighting she refers to is that of honest dialogue in which the couple sort out their differences by listening and responding to each other. For example, when they get angry with each other they may either refuse to talk about it, in which case their relationship will most likely deteriorate, or they may decide to talk it out in an honest fashion in the belief that this will lead to a better relationship. They experience for themselves the truth of the saying that a relationship is as good as the communication going on within it. The truth of this saying is born out by the fact that communication or conversation is the most effective as well as the most practical way of growing in intimacy.

Conversation is innate to the way we relate

We have already noted that the listening and responding essential to conversation are built into the four levels at which we relate and become intimate. At the sensate level we recall the events of our story and in doing so become receptive or adopt a listening stance to our experience. When we listen to the events of our story it is likely that our feelings will be aroused and these feelings are of their nature a response to what we are listening to in our story. At the third or intuitive level of our experience, where we glimpse the significance of what has been happening to us in the events of our story, we again become receptive or again adopt our listening stance. Finally, at the fourth level of our experience our convictions about what is of value are the source of the deepest feelings out of which we respond to our experience.

The most effective way to intimacy

As well as conversation being innate to each of the four levels at which we relate, or become intimate, it is the essential means by which we move from one of these levels of intimacy to another. For example, the most effective way of converting the intuitive glimpses we get at the third level into the convictions at the fourth is by listening and responding to them. If we are to assimilate the glimpses of our true self which others give us we will find no more effective way than by listening to them. Similarly, responding to or saying how we feel about these glimpses reinforces them, and it also helps us to overcome the resistance we may feel to these positive glimpses we get of ourselves. Thus conversation is the most effective way to become intimate with others, because by it we get in touch with and share our inmost self with others.

The most practical way to intimacy

As well as conversation being the most effective, it is also the most practical way to foster intimacy. Good communication does more than anything else to bring about a union of minds and hearts. We experience this when we reflect on the effect that being listened to has on us. Those who listen to us and draw us out not only help us to articulate what is meaningful and worthwhile for us, but give us a sense of being accepted and appreciated. This creates a deep bond with those who listen to us. Likewise, when people respond to us in an affirming way, it makes it easier for us to express our feelings. This mutual sharing of feelings does much for intimacy, as we saw in chapter 8.

The effect of listening and responding to others

We also foster intimacy in a most practical way when we are the ones who listen and respond in conversation. There are few things that encourage the self-disclosure in which intimacy consists than listening and responding to others. When we listen to them we open ourselves to how they see things and feel about them and this encourages them to disclose more and more of themselves. When we respond honestly to what we have heard others say, it can be very reassuring for them when our response is positive. It gives them a sense that it is safe to share the very intimate part of themselves that their feelings reveal.

What is probably the most important effect of genuine conversation is the implicit expression that it gives to attitudes which underlie it. These attitudes of sensitivity, respect, acceptance, appreciation and concern, that underlie the way friends listen and respond to each other, make our intimate relationships so life-giving.

The Exercise

The aim of this exercise is to highlight how effective and practical conversation is in cultivating intimacy.

1. From your experience of the TV you watch, or the films you go to, say what you think is the main effect of our failure to communicate? Give one reason why the art of conversation is so neglected when the benefits of it are so great. What is the most striking thing you notice about the way most people communicate or fail to communicate in your family or at work?

2. Remember someone who was good at listening to you in an attentive and sympathetic way and notice how the memory of this experience effects you. Do the same with an experience you have had of someone who was good at responding honestly to what you said. Think of a person whom you listen to and then respond honestly to, and say what effect it has on this person and what effect it has on you.

3. Reflect back on your life and notice if there were people you met along the way who were good conversationalists? What was it about the way one of them engaged you in conversation that you admired? What are some of the ways people carry on a conversation that annoy you? If you were asked to choose three guidelines for developing the art of conversation, what would they be?

4. Tell the story of one close relationship you have had. After noting down how you see and feel about the role of this person in your life, enter a conversation with him or her. When you have finished the conversation describe one effect of being listened and responded honestly to and one effect of listening and responding to the other person.

PART 5

The call to be generative

Answering the call to become generative
requires that we keep expanding
the scope of our relationships.
We seek to befriend more and more people and things,
especially those we have become estranged from.

The call to become

Generative

is a call to expand the circle

of our sensitivity and concern

to include more and more

people and things in it

An Outline of Part 5

In Part 5 we look at how we answer the third call of adult life by becoming generative.

In Chapter 19 we see that being generative involves expanding our horizons of who and what we are sensitive and responsive to. To do this we focus on three dimensions of people and things, their wonder and indispensable role in our life, their being our companions as well as signs of a deeper reality.

In Chapter 20 we seek to befriend all those people and areas of our lives from which we have become estranged by opening a dialogue with them.

CHAPTER 19

Expanding the horizons of our concern

Becoming generative means expanding our horizons
to incorporate more and more people and things
into the circle of who and what we are concerned for.
We do this by entering a conversation with each of them
as wondrous, as a companion and as a symbol of a deeper reality

No man is an island, entire of itself;
every man is a piece of a continent, a part of the main; …
any man's death diminishes me, because I am involved in mankind.
and therefore never send to know for whom the bell tolls;
it tolls for thee
John Donne

Becoming *generative*

involves expanding our horizons

of *understanding* and *concern*

Very often the motivation for answering the call to become generative is compassion. Our heart goes out to others who are in need of
our help. Life invites us, as it did the Buddha, to keep expanding
the circle of people and things we are sensitive to and concerned
about.

How Buddha learned compassion

At the beginning of his life, even though the Buddha had an
abundance of this world's goods he was not happy. His parents
did their best to shield him from life's hardships. They even had
the inside of the windows of his carriage painted with pleasant
pictures so that he might not witness the pain of the world
around him.

Then one day when he was travelling through his kingdom
he opened the window of his carriage and saw the Four Sights.
He saw people who were hungry looking for food, he saw others
who were mourning a loss, he became aware of sickness and of
how people faced old age. These sights had such a profound
effect on him that he left his kingdom and went on a journey in
search of enlightenment. He eventually found it under the Bo
Tree where he was inspired to become a Buddha for others. As a
result, wherever we go we find statues of the Buddha. He is
smiling, for having learned compassion he is at home with the
joys and sorrows of all humanity.

Expanding our horizons

Like the Buddha, we are challenged to be sensitive and responsive
to what is happening around us. As children we may be oblivious to
what others are going through, but as we grow up we feel drawn to
become more sensitive and compassionate towards others, we are
challenged to keep expanding the horizons of our understanding
and of our concern. While the invitation to become generative is
initially experienced in our relationship with people, we are invited
to extend it to everything that forms part of our environment. In
practice becoming generative involves learning to relate with everyone and everything as a source of wonder, as a companion and as a
symbol of a deeper reality.

A source of wonder

Becoming generative towards people or things means befriending them in the sense that we acknowledge them or become more sensitive and respectful towards them. For example, if we want to be more generative towards our body, we need to become more sensitive to some of the ways our body plays an indispensable role in our life. For instance, we might imagine how we would feel if we were deprived of our body's capacity to see or hear, how limited we would be without our eyes. We can also befriend our body by cultivating a sense of respect for it by spending time in wonder, for example, at how our hands can perform the most intricate activities with such skill.

A lifelong companion

Becoming generative towards or befriending any part of ourselves or our environment involves cultivating an acceptance and an appreciation of it as our lifelong companion. Ira Progoff in his book, *At an Intensive Journal Workshop*, suggests that we do this by initiating a dialogue. He recommends that we prepare for this by telling the story of our relationship with our body or with leisure, and after making a brief statement about where the relationship is now, he recommends that we enter into a dialogue with it, writing out both sides of this in full.

A symbol of a deeper reality

Becoming generative also involves developing our awareness of how everything can put us in touch with our inner world. For the poet, in each of us 'Earth's crammed with heaven, And every bush is afire with God' (E. B. Browning). The simplest flower can put us in touch with its deepest self and with our own.

The Exercise

The aim of this exercise is to help you to understand the meaning of the call to become generative and how you might answer it.

1. What recent issues reported in the news concern you most? What way do you react when some of these issues disappear from the attention of the media so quickly? If you were a journalist, what would be your main area of concern? What do you admire most about people like Mother Theresa and Bob Geldof or about groups like Greenpeace and Amnesty International?

2. How would you describe the call to become generative to someone who had never heard of it before? After listing some of the ways you see yourself called to be generative, choose one that appeals to you. Describe when this experience of the call to become generative first became important for you and list a few key moments in the development of the way you have sought to answer this call.

3. What kinds of people do you find yourself most concerned about? Draw a diagram with a number of circles, one inside the other. To get a sense of the relative importance of your concerns about people and the environment, place the most important ones in the centre circle and the others in the circles surrounding this in the order of their importance for you. List some of the ways you would like to help people and describe one way you actually try to help them. Are there people you would like to be more concerned about? How does your inability or powerlessness to help people, who for example have been bereaved, make you feel?

4. Is there a group of people from whom you feel estranged? What is the cause of this estrangement and how do you feel about it? What way of seeing these people and what ways of behaving towards them do you notice yourself adopting? If you wanted to improve your relationship with these people, how would you go about it?

CHAPTER 20

Befriending what we are estranged from

Being generative involves befriending areas of our world
we have become estranged from,
by engaging each of them in a dialogue.

Compassion is not sloppy, sentimental feeling for people
who are underprivileged or sick … it is an absolutely
practical belief that, regardless of a person's background,
ability, or ability to pay, he should be provided with the best
that society has to offer.
Neil Kinnock

Befriending the estranged

Our body and sexuality	Our soul
What we need to befriend	
Work and leisure	nature, technology and the environment

In chapter 19 we looked at the third call of adult life which is the call to become generative. We saw how this is a call to gradually befriend everyone and everything in our environment. In this chapter we will examine what we can do about people and areas of our lives we have become estranged from. This state of estrangement may be due to the fact that a conflict with someone has never been resolved or it may be due to the fact that we have not established or maintained a relationship with some area of our environment.

The tendency to restrict our horizons of understanding and concern, and so to become estranged from large areas of the world in which we live, is symbolised for us in the myth of the Great Warrior.

The myth of the great warrior

We grow up believing that we live in a hostile world in which we term the bulk of people we are not on familiar terms with as 'them' and those we are close to as 'us'. The need to defend ourselves against those we think of as 'them' breeds the mentality of the great warrior. This mentality gradually limits the scope of our understanding and concern to a small group of people and we tend to adopt a cold or an impersonal attitude towards the rest.

The scope of our understanding and concern or compassion is limited still further by attitudes generated by this myth. For example, its belief that the feminine side of each of us does not belong to the great warrior ethos leads to a lack of understanding of and respect for large areas of life. The fact that qualities such as sensitivity, tenderness and compassion are regarded as unbecoming the more rugged *esprit de corps* of the great warrior has a limiting effect on our relationships. This myth also generates a very poor relationship with our environment as it easily justifies a ruthless exploitation of it for commercial interests.

The disaster of modernity

The fact that today we are out of touch with much of our inner world is so serious that Ken Wilber, in his book *The Marriage of Sense and Soul,* calls it 'the disaster of modernity'. The source of this disaster is to be found in the way that science, economics and our consumer culture has so emphasised the importance of the exterior world of material things that it has marginalised the interior world of relationships.

What we wish to do in this chapter is to develop a way of establishing and maintaining a relationship with the many parts of our inner world from which we have become estranged. Examples of areas we are estranged from are evident in the poor relationship many of us have with our body, with our sexuality and with our soul. We may notice too that we have a poor relationship with leisure, with work, with nature and with the environment in which we live.

Befriending what we are estranged from
The call to be generative invites us to gradually befriend these areas from which we have become estranged. If we take our body as an example, befriending it involves finding a way to draw it into the circle of intimacy we have found with ourselves and with others. This means cultivating a new attitude to our body by acknowledging how useful and wondrous it is, by accepting its limitations and our own, in that we may have neglected or abused it. Cultivating this new attitude to our body also involves appreciating what a good companion it has always been, as well as developing a deep concern for its welfare.

A practical way of befriending or establishing a healthy relationship with our body, for example, involves the following steps:
- Telling the story of our relationship with our body
- Saying where this relationship is now
- Entering a dialogue

The Exercise

The aim of this exercise is to develop a way of befriending or of re-establishing a relationship with all those areas of yourself and of your environment from which you have become estranged.

1. Is there a protest song about the way we are damaging or destroying any part of our environment that you identify with? Briefly tell the story of a novel or a film, like *Gorillas In The Mist,* about the shameful abuse of some area of our environment. A lot of people pay lip-service to the conservation of the environment but do not do anything about it. What stance do you adopt? What do you try to do about it? Choose a picture and a caption about our responsibility for our environment that you identify with.

2. Name some areas of your life, perhaps from those mentioned in the introduction to this exercise, from which you have become cut off or estranged. Take one of these areas and describe how you have become estranged from it through lack of awareness of its importance, for example. Is there a way of going about befriending this area that appeals to you?

3. Recall an incident when you became concerned about some part of your environment that you felt was being damaged. What way did the stance you adopted in this case alter your views on and your feelings about this area of your environment which you felt was threatened?

There are three aspects of everything in your environment that may help you to clarify how you see and feel about it. We will reflect on these in the final three parts of this exercise.

4. Choose an area of your environment, like water, and notice the various ways it is useful or even indispensable for you. To get a sense of what life would be like without uncontaminated water, imagine that you have been told that within a year a lake or river you treasure will be so contaminated that nothing will live in it any more. Notice how you feel about the prospect of this loss. Next, give yourself time to marvel at the wonder of water and at how all life depends on it.

5. To establish a personal relationship with some aspect of your environment that you value highly enter into a dialogue with it as you would with a friend. Begin by outlining the story of your relationship with something like music, by recalling some significant events in the development of your relationship with it. After describing what music means to you now, enter a dialogue in which you listen and talk to each other as friends do. Write out the main thing that you wish to say to each other as a result of your conversation.

6. A dimension of everything in the world around you that you need to befriend is its capacity to inspire you or put you in touch with an inner reality. Take an example of something like a piece of music, a song, a work of art or something like Tennyson's 'flower in the crannie wall' and describe what it inspires in you or the inner reality it can put you in touch with.

The Call to Wisdom

Answering the call to wisdom involves
developing an intimate knowledge
of the love we have received and given
within life's basic relationships.

Wisdom
is *today's experience*
seen in the light of *yesterday's*
and both of these seen in the light of
experience common to us all

An Outline of Part 6

Part 6 has one chapter in which we look at the fourth call of adult life, the call to wisdom. This call is to discover, explore and to make our own of a unique inner wisdom which each of us possesses. This wisdom is an interior knowledge springing from a lifetime's experience of the love we have received and shared within the relationships which make up our inner world.

CHAPTER 21

The fruit of a lifetime's relationships

Wisdom is the fruit of a lifetime's experience,
an interior knowledge, derived from
the love received and given
at the four levels at which we relate

Knowledge dwells in heads replete with thoughts of other men,
wisdom in minds attentive to their own
William Cowper

Wisdom
is an *intimate knowledge*
of the love we receive and give
at the four levels
at which we conduct all our relationships

For much of our life we may be unaware of something precious that we have gradually accumulated. This is often the case with the wisdom we have gained from the main relationships of our lives. It is not immediately obvious that we possess this wisdom as it runs through our lives like an underground stream. Thus the fourth call of adult life is to get in touch with and gradually take possession of the precious jewel we have in this wisdom.

In search of the Priceless Jewel

There was once a young man on a journey who because of a storm was forced to take refuge in a cave. As he wandered into the inner recesses of the cave he discovered a precious jewel the beauty of which enthralled him. However, all he could do was to gaze at the jewel as it was guarded by a ferocious beast which did not allow him to do more than look at the jewel from a distance. When eventually he left the cave to continue his journey he knew that his life's quest would be to take possession of this jewel.

In due time he married and reared a family and then, when his life's work was done and much of his dream realised, he said to his wife, 'Before I die, I must again glimpse and perhaps take possession of the jewel that has been the inspiration of my life.' So he set out and made his way back to the cave where he again found the jewel. But now the beast guarding it had grown so old that he was able to take the jewel away with him. As he made his way back home, the meaning of his lifelong quest for the jewel gradually dawned on him. He realised that life had taught him a precious wisdom that he was only now ready to take possession of.

We accumulate the wisdom that is symbolised by this precious jewel so gradually that it tends to remain unnoticed. This is unless we learn to become aware of and take responsibility for making our own of the jewel we have in life's accumulated wisdom. One of the reasons why it is generally late in life before we answer the call to do this is that our appreciation of the importance of this kind of wisdom takes a long time to mature.

Different views of wisdom

Initially, we may think of wisdom as a deep intellectual grasp of some area of knowledge. Then, as we become acquainted with our inner world, wisdom may come to be defined in terms of the skill with which we handle the relationships central to this inner world.

At some stage we may become aware of how central to our relationships is the love, the concern, the care or the compassion that holds these relationships together. Wisdom then becomes a lifetime's experience of the love we give and receive. We gradually realise that the love we give is 'wide-eyed' or perceptive in that it is sensitive to the best way to relate and to the art of loving.

The wisdom which comes from loving is only surpassed by the wisdom we learn from those who love us, from the vision we see in their eyes. This intimate knowledge of being loved, of being acknowledged, accepted and affirmed is the deepest wisdom as it is what effects us most profoundly. Like Care, it is what makes and sustains us throughout life.

Wisdom as an interior knowledge

Our view of wisdom will be deeply influenced by whether we see it mainly as an exterior knowledge that emerges from our mind or as an interior knowledge that emerges from the four levels at which we relate. Wisdom as an interior knowledge is a vision of ourselves and of others which we gradually pick up within our relationships. It is a wisdom derived as much from the heart as from the head, from the senses as much as from the intuitive side of ourselves.

> Enlightenment is not an idea but the way another person looks at you. (Henry de Lubac)

Unfortunately, the wisdom we derive from these four levels at which we relate is largely dormant, or part of what we have called our underground stream of inner wisdom. It remains dormant because we do not make time to reflect on the intimate knowledge we have accumulated from our experience of relating with others and from 'the way they look at us'. However, we catch a glimpse of how extensive and profound this wisdom is when, for example, we reflect on all that we learn from our experience of rearing a child. If we are to answer the fourth call of adult life, we need to find a way of accessing our stream of inner wisdom and of making our own of the vast amount of wisdom available to us there.

Owning our wisdom

To arouse, to savour and to own our dormant wisdom we need to relive the significant experiences of the story of the relationships which have influenced us most. Next we need to notice and put words on the feelings, the glimpses and the convictions which arise as we tell the story of the love we have received and given within these relationships. It is in the light of this wisdom that unfolds in the course of our whole story that we are able to notice and appreciate the wisdom that emerges in our daily experience. This fund of personal wisdom is greatly enhanced when reflected on in the light of a more universal wisdom. This is the wisdom expressed in other people's stories which is made available to us in many forms such as novels and plays, films and biographies.

The greatest work of art

The wisdom which gradually emerges from our relationships, and from the love we receive and give within them, can be compared to the gift of an uncut jewel or diamond we receive at birth. Our life's work is to cut and polish this diamond so that we gradually realise its potential, the many facets of its splendour. This effort to realise the splendour of the diamond symbolises our lifelong effort to become skilled in the way we relate with ourselves and others, in the way we give and receive the Care that makes and sustains us. This is the main work of art we are each commissioned with and none can surpass it in importance and in beauty.

The Exercise

The aim of this exercise is to understand the fourth call of adult life, the call to wisdom, and how you might go about answering it.

1. Think of some people who embody an idea of wisdom that you identify with. Name three of these and describe an aspect of the wisdom of each of them that you admire. How is the kind of

wisdom that you find most attractive expressed among people you associate with at present?

2. As you think of your parents, what do you consider characterised their wisdom? What parts of their vision and values, or of their convictions about what is true and worthwhile, do you find most appealing? Name an area of their wisdom that you do not feel drawn to or for which you have substituted your own.

3. Which of the following three areas of your life has contributed most to your wisdom: your work, your marriage or rearing your children? What is the most striking piece of wisdom that this area of your life has taught you?

4. Describe one experience which contributed a lot to the wisdom life has taught you. What feelings are aroused when you remember this experience? Can you put words on what is significant about this experience or what it is saying to you? If what you learned from this experience triggers off a deep conviction about what is true and worthwhile in life, say what this conviction is. Is the wisdom you learned from this experience part of a wider or more universal experience that an image, a piece of poetry or a story captures in an imaginative way for you?

5. Pay a visit to someone who is a wisdom figure in your life or to an imaginary person who fills this role for you. As you journey to meet this person reflect on what part of your wisdom you want to talk about and when you meet share your thoughts and feelings about this. As you make your way home take time to write down what is the main piece of wisdom you have become aware of in this conversation with your wisdom figure.

6. List five to ten areas of your experience where you have learned something that is an important part of your wisdom. Draw a large circle in which the part of this vision that is most meaningful and attractive for you is placed at the centre. Around this, place the other aspects of your wisdom in the order of their importance for you.